T0312290

Cambridge Elements ≡

Elements in Applied Social Psychology
edited by
Susan Clayton
College of Wooster, Ohio

BEHAVIORAL INSIGHTS FOR PUBLIC POLICY

Contextualizing Our Science

Crystal C. Hall
University of Washington

Ines Jurcevic
University of Washington

CAMBRIDGE
UNIVERSITY PRESS

CAMBRIDGE
UNIVERSITY PRESS

University Printing House, Cambridge CB2 8BS, United Kingdom

One Liberty Plaza, 20th Floor, New York, NY 10006, USA

477 Williamstown Road, Port Melbourne, VIC 3207, Australia

314–321, 3rd Floor, Plot 3, Splendor Forum, Jasola District Centre,
New Delhi – 110025, India

103 Penang Road, #05–06/07, Visioncrest Commercial, Singapore 238467

Cambridge University Press is part of the University of Cambridge.

It furthers the University's mission by disseminating knowledge in the pursuit of
education, learning, and research at the highest international levels of excellence.

www.cambridge.org
Information on this title: www.cambridge.org/9781009013918
DOI: 10.1017/9781009028806

© Crystal C. Hall and Ines Jurcevic 2022

First published 2022

A catalogue record for this publication is available from the British Library.

ISBN 978-1-009-01391-8 Paperback
ISSN 2631-777X (online)
ISSN 2631-7761 (print)

Additional resources for this publication at www.cambridge.org/publicpolicy

Behavioral Insights for Public Policy

Contextualizing Our Science

Elements in Applied Social Psychology

DOI: 10.1017/9781009028806
First published online: April 2022

Crystal C. Hall
University of Washington

Ines Jurcevic
University of Washington

Author for correspondence: Crystal C. Hall, hallcc@uw.edu

Abstract: There has been an increasing effort to integrate behavioral insights into public policy. These insights are often reliant on social psychological research and theory. However, in this relatively young field, policy interventions and behavioral insights are often built on laboratory-based psychological research, with effects that can prove to be unstable in the "real world." In this Element, the authors provide a brief history of how behavioral insights have been applied to complex policy problems. They describe ways in which behavioral insights have been successful and where they have fallen short. In addition, they examine unintended negative consequences of nudges and provide a more nuanced examination of their impacts on behavior change. Finally, the Element concludes with a set of recommendations for generating more effective practical applications of psychology to the field of public policy.

Keywords: behavioral insights, equity, nudging, psychological tax, public policy

ISBNs: 9781009013918 (PB), 9781009028806 (OC)
ISSNs: 2631-777X (online), 2631-7761 (print)

Contents

1 Overview

A growing body of evidence demonstrates that behavioral science insights – research findings from fields such as behavioral economics and psychology about how people make decisions and act on them – can be used to design government policies to better serve the American people.

Where Federal policies have been designed to reflect behavioral science insights, they have substantially improved outcomes for the individuals, families, communities, and businesses those policies serve. For example, automatic enrollment and automatic escalation in retirement savings plans have made it easier to save for the future, and have helped Americans accumulate billions of dollars in additional retirement savings. Similarly, streamlining the application process for Federal financial aid has made college more financially accessible for millions of students.

To more fully realize the benefits of behavioral insights and deliver better results at a lower cost for the American people, the Federal Government should design its policies and programs to reflect our best understanding of how people engage with, participate in, use, and respond to those policies and programs. By improving the effectiveness and efficiency of Government, behavioral science insights can support a range of national priorities, including helping workers to find better jobs; enabling Americans to lead longer, healthier lives; improving access to educational opportunities and support for success in school; and accelerating the transition to a low-carbon economy.

—Executive Order No. 13,707: *Using Behavioral Science Insights to Better Serve the American People*. Signed by President Barack H. Obama on September 15, 2015

In recent decades, psychology and public policy have begun to merge in an unprecedented way. Researchers have worked hand in hand with policy practitioners to improve the design, implementation, and evaluation of public policy. The opening excerpt acknowledges the evidence provided by the field of psychology and sets up a directive to federal agencies in the United States to consider the incorporation of such behavioral insights into their work. It specifically mentions the need for the federal government to design programs and policies that reflect our best understanding of how people engage and make decisions – and social psychology has the disciplinary expertise, influence, and imperative to improve that understanding. While this institutionalization of behavioral insights in government does not represent the first effort of its type, it was certainly one of the most high-profile and wide-ranging in the United States, and similar efforts have been incorporated into government and public institution initiatives globally.

Critically, in this relatively young field, policy interventions and behavioral insights have relied on theory and findings that stem from social psychology. As such, they are commonly built on laboratory-based psychological research, with effects that are often subtle and unstable in the messy and multifaceted real world of public policy. There is substantial opportunity and need to expand and refine the way that psychological research is produced in order to better enable research and discipline to be more equitably leveraged in applied research and practitioner domains and enable a more inclusive science. Indeed, as one example, the American Psychological Association (APA) guidelines explicitly call on researchers to be "aware of the critical role of science in informing practice and policy and therefore strive to conduct and disseminate research that promotes the well-being of racial and ethnic minorities" (APA, 2019a, p. 27). The APA offers similar guidelines for considering the impact of psychological research on other underrepresented or marginalized communities. Ultimately, this recalibration will allow for psychological science to authentically work in the service of the public good – a goal shared by many, if not most, scholars of the discipline.

In Section 2 of this Element, we offer a definition and explore the history of behavioral insights, with an emphasis on nudging: A nudge is any aspect of a decision context that has an impact on people's behavior, without removing any decision paths. Behavioral insights, and nudges in particular, have been celebrated as cheap and easy tools to improve efficiency and the cost-effectiveness of outcomes. In the sections that follow, we provide the history and context for several of these successful applications of behavioral insights.

Subsequently, we engage the shortfalls of behavioral insights and contend that the implementation of these insights is built on psychological research that often does not account for, or de-emphasizes, individual difference and distributional effects stemming from personality traits, race, class, and other sociodemographic and cultural factors. In the diverse domains of public policy, it is critical to explore the nuances of these behavioral effects – how and when they operate – in order to engage equity, in addition to efficiency and cost-effectiveness. When we consider the use of these behavioral insight tools by governments and other entities that advocate for and impact a large and diverse set of constituents, the general assumption to date that a small net benefit occurs over a large population is insufficient and can result in inequitable and unethical practices and outcomes. This is particularly true given the broad interest in sustainable and scalable innovations based on insights from psychology. We contend that scholars of social and personality psychology are particularly well-suited to address these gaps in the research and must acknowledge (and account for) several factors in the design of their research.

We propose that the question of whether nudges succeed or fail is far more complicated than what has been examined to date. There are critical equity implications of this limitation. Existing efforts place disproportionate emphasis on whether the desired or hypothesized behavior change occurs (deemed a success) or does not occur (deemed a failure). For "failed" nudges, researchers consider either no behavioral change or behavioral reactance as failures and generally refocus on adjusting and reapplying psychological tools to change behavior. We propose that psychologists have not focused deeply enough on attempts to integrate the nuanced richness of social psychology into efforts to apply the insights from this field. This is true for scholars across the spectrum of social psychology – those who examine individual differences in decision-making and social cognition and those engaging intergroup, cultural, and social meaning-making processes. Nudges have the potential to carry with them additional psychological costs, and these costs are not always distributed equally. Unlocking the relatively untapped potential of social psychology can help scholars and practitioners begin to unpack and understand these costs.

We articulate some of these consequences and their broader implications for examining and developing equitable research practices and applications. First, we provide an overview and evidence for the psycho-emotional tax that behavioral interventions have the potential to carry. Here, we contend that in addition to examining behavior change, nudges and behavioral insights applications should, in parallel, examine the meaningful costs of stigma, negative emotion activation, and cognitive depletion. Second, we propose that considering these psycho-emotional taxes enables researchers and practitioners to better understand who is being helped or harmed by particular types of nudges, and thereby avoid approaches that provide a disproportionate benefit to those who are relatively better off. Here, we define "better off" as individuals who have the psychological, financial, temporal, or other resources to better reap the benefits of nudges. Third, we call for better data to promote better outcomes for the public good. We underscore the critical importance of disaggregating data and examining behavioral and psychological effects in social psychological research as well as a need to collect data in the wild (i.e., outside of the lab) to enable social psychology to engage with public policy meaningfully and responsibly, with the aim of promoting equitable, in addition to efficient and cost-effective, insights.

Social and personality psychology will be critical for developing a more nuanced understanding of both the behavioral and psychological impacts of behavioral insights approaches and applications. These implications will come alongside a process of developing insights that are better suited to a diverse array of social contexts to which social psychology is being applied. This type of approach to designing and implementing research – one that emphasizes intentionally examining behavioral and psychological outcomes across heterogeneous and diverse samples and contexts – will have significant positive implications for developing equitable behavioral interventions in psychology and across applied domains. This Element provides concrete recommendations for how the field can contribute in this space.

2 Background: A Brief History of Nudging and Applied Behavioral Insights

2.1 "Nudge" Defined

First, we review and discuss a brief history of nudging and the evolution of the field of applied behavioral insights. In the literal sense, the definition of "nudge" is to gently touch or push an item or a person. A nudge can be employed to gain a person's attention or direct their attention in a particular direction. In the world of behavioral insights, the use of the term "nudge" closely follows this literal definition. Richard Thaler and Cass Sunstein popularized the term and use the following definition at the start of their pioneering work, *Nudge*:

> A nudge, as we will use the term, is any aspect of the choice architecture that alters people's behavior in a predictable way without forbidding any options or significantly changing their economic incentives. To count as a mere nudge, the intervention must be easy and cheap to avoid. Nudges are not mandates. Putting fruit at eye level counts as a nudge. Banning junk food does not. (Thaler & Sunstein, 2009, p. 6)

Critical in this definition is that the intervention must be subtle. In other words, a nudge as opposed to a shove. While this definition has been widely adopted in both academic circles and the popular press, others have attempted to refine the idea. For example, one paper argues that the true definition of a nudge has become a bit confused and attempts to clarify the definition of a nudge (thereby hoping to increase the value of the idea) by revisiting the corresponding foundations in the field of behavioral economics (Hansen, 2016). Hansen more specifically defines a nudge as follows:

> A nudge is a function of (I) any attempt at influencing people's judgment, choice or behavior in a predictable way (1) that is motivated because of cognitive boundaries, biases, routines, and habits in individual and social decision-making posing barriers for people to perform rationally in their own self-declared interests, and which (2) works by making use of those boundaries, biases, routines, and habits as integral parts of such attempts.
>
> (Hansen, 2016, p. 158)

Hansen argues that this definition allows for a more foundational understanding of what it means to engage in this type of influence on behavior. Thaler and Sunstein's original definition essentially serves as a description of the outcomes that result from Hansen's. Nudges may operate separately from regulation and mandates, but they need not be required to do so. It is crucial to note, however, that this definition is not the only recent reconceptualization that has been put forth. One earlier critique argues that many nudges are not truly paternalistic but rather demonstrate persuasion that is arguably rational (Hausman & Welch, 2010). A second posits that nudging is an example of a specific form of governance that can be employed by a policymaker (as opposed to the other four that exist: "hierarchy," "markets," "networks," and "persuasion"). It argues that, typically, nudging does not create sustained behavior change – this would more likely be achieved by promoting social identity and norm changes (Mols et al., 2015). Ultimately, these authors all stress that scholars and practitioners of public policy ought to more diligently consider individuals as complex members of social groups rather than individual actors with cognitive limitations. These two thoughtful approaches are important to note because they underscore the value in considering the philosophical and practical nuance in alternative conceptualizations of this idea. We also acknowledge that it has been disputed as to whether "nudge theory" represents a new approach to behavior change or a reframing of prior efforts to do so. As mentioned, there are worthy arguments about the proper definition (and utility) of nudging, and these perspectives carry implications for both research and practical application of these approaches to social problems.

For our purposes, we apply a straightforward definition of nudging that we believe captures the initial spirit of Thaler and Sunstein's definition, incorporates some of the subtle nuance offered by Hansen and Mols, and allows for an interpretation that has value to scholars and practitioners alike. It is not our intent to enter into the debate regarding the most appropriate definition of nudges. We consider a nudge to be an element of a choice environment that has the potential to alter an individual's behavior (whether or not it is intended to do so). This environmental feature must not change the options or decision paths available to the decision maker and must not change the incentives present (economic or otherwise).

2.2 Nudging Rises to Prominence

In the early 2000s, several lines of research and other notable events came together to bring the field of psychology to the forefront of popular discussion in an unprecedented way. In 2001, a seminal paper demonstrated that a shift from an opt-in to an opt-out process significantly impacted retirement savings (Madrian & Shea, 2001). This paper performed an analysis of automatic enrollment into 401(k) savings plans. Two crucial findings emerged from this work: first, participation in a 401(k) program was higher when workers were automatically enrolled; second, many participants who were automatically enrolled kept the default for both rate of contribution and allocation of funds in their account. The authors argue that the tendency of participants to stick to the defaults reflects psychological inertia and a belief that the default provides advice on how to manage the retirement investments. These findings illuminate the reality that behavioral factors may weigh heavily on economic decision-making and provide strong implications for how these types of accounts ought to be managed. More broadly, they also connect to the importance of how defaults are designed and what these decisions communicate when deployed in the public sector – with recent research highlighting that defaults are seen as communicating policymaker preferences and recommendations (McKenzie et al., 2006). Ultimately, Madrian and Shea's work led to the Pension Protection Act, which is discussed in Section 2.3.

The following year, Daniel Kahneman was awarded the 2002 Nobel Prize in Economic Science for his work with Amos Tversky (sadly, Tversky passed away in 1996, prior to this recognition). Together, Kahneman and Tversky provided fundamental challenges to the role that the assumption of rationality had played in modern economic theory. They established evidence on a wide range of cognitive biases that stem from bounded rationality, as originally defined by Herbert Simon (1957). Tversky and Kahneman brought together the fields of psychology and economics in a way not previously accomplished, and they rooted this work in their observations of real-world behavioral puzzles. Specifically, their extensive work provided insights on judgment under uncertainty. Their studies laid the foundation for what was a new field of research, changing the course and influence of scholarship in both economics and psychology. One of their most prominent contributions, Prospect Theory (Kahneman & Tversky, 1979), incorporated psychological insights as a descriptive theory of choice (compared to Expected Utility Theory from economics) and continues to be applied to real-world decision-making in diverse contexts ranging from labor economics to gambling behavior to decisions about residential movement (Camerer, 1998; Clark & Lisowski, 2017). Kahneman and Tversky's long friendship and evolution of their work are explored in compelling detail in Michael Lewis' popular press book *The Undoing Project* (Lewis, 2016).

In 2003, two papers that proved foundational to the amplification of applied behavioral insights were published. Johnson and Goldstein (2003) demonstrated the impact of defaults on decision-making in the context of organ donation rates and made a convincing argument for how policymakers ought to approach the framing of important practical choices. Specifically, they argue that every policy action must have a default specified that will be engaged if no active choice is made. Defaults impose costs (be they physical, cognitive, and/or emotional) on individuals who must change their status and, as such, must be carefully considered and articulated. Furthermore, they note that the "costs" of switching are sometimes imposed on the group that appears to be in the majority. If the majority of individuals in a society favor organ donation (as measured, in this case, by both a national study and results of the experiment), policies that require active consent are placing the switching costs on the largest group of individuals, potentially amplifying those costs. This was the case in the United States. At the time of this study, the majority of individuals in the United States favored organ donation, and at the same time, many states also had an opt-in organ donation policy, creating decision friction for the dominant opinion. This simple study goes far to illustrate the need for the design and implementation of public policies to carefully consider these costs and the role of defaults.

These findings dovetail nicely with arguments made in "Libertarian paternalism" (Thaler & Sunstein, 2003). This influential paper introduced the concept of libertarian paternalism – "an approach that preserves freedom of choice but that authorizes both private and public institutions to steer people in directions that will promote their welfare" (Thaler & Sunstein, 2003, p. 179). Further, they describe the misunderstandings associated with the concept of paternalism and aim to clarify why it should not be considered a "derogatory" term. Critically, the authors point out that (1) there are often not good alternatives to paternalism, as choice architects are sometimes forced to make decisions on behalf of those who will choose (and often do not want to do so randomly), and (2) paternalism does not always have to involve coercion. In addition, they describe tools that can be used to create a good system of choice. They contend that libertarian paternalism is an option that can preserve individual freedom of choice while simultaneously steering people in the direction that promotes their well-being, and it is often described as a form of *soft* paternalism – meaning paternalism that does not restrict freedom of choice. For example, a government that attempts to curb smoking by mandating images and language regarding diseases caused by tobacco is engaging in soft paternalism. An outright ban on tobacco by the government goes beyond this type of intervention, falling more squarely into the category of outright paternalism.

In their book *Nudge* (first published in 2008), Thaler and Sunstein provide an expansion of their arguments on libertarian paternalism. Specifically, they lay out the principles of effective choice architecture. The existence or nonexistence of a default option is one important point of consideration, but other factors such as the number of options presented and the way that information is described are important features. Thaler and Sunstein use the System I (quick, unconscious, intuitive processes) versus the System II (slow, conscious, deliberative processes) framework and describe how it leads to many predictable behavioral biases. Ultimately, this leads to policy recommendations (their focus is primarily in the areas of retirement savings and health care/health outcomes). More of the scholarly history of the field of behavioral economics is outlined in Thaler's *Misbehaving* (Thaler, 2016) and many of the important fundamental psychological insights are described in Daniel Kahneman's *Thinking, Fast and Slow* (Kahneman, 2011).

Importantly, while the concept of libertarian paternalism as an intervention approach has received substantial support, it has also received significant criticism. These criticisms have been well developed and articulated by numerous psychologists, legal scholars, economists, political scientists, and philosophers over the decades (e.g., Ewert, 2020; Schmidt & Engelen, 2020). For example, scholars have cautioned that there are clear power dynamics that need to be considered with regard to which entities and individuals are in the privileged position to nudge others' behavior and who is in the lower power position of receiving that nudge. This has implications for the types of nudges that are seen as normative and desirable and has the potential to reify social hierarchies and devaluation of lower status identities, thereby impacting well-being across many metrics. It is a consideration that is particularly relevant to government and public policy, where opting out of engaging with the "nudger" is near impossible given the ubiquitous role of the government in daily life. Moreover, when errors in soft paternalism occur and an entity inadvertently guides individuals to a less desirable decision or behavior, who bears those costs and who corrects for those errors? Because these concerns have been substantially engaged over the last decade, we do not do so here. Rather, these considerations are seeds to the novel concerns we raise in Section 4. For now, we consider the celebrated successes of behavioral insights applications, emphasizing their efficiency and cost-effectiveness.

2.3 Public Policy Applications of Behavioral Insights

Next, we detail the applications of behavioral insights to public policy contexts, focusing on efforts to promote efficacy and efficiency, as these have been of primary emphasis to date. Given author expertise, we initially emphasize policy applications in the United States but clarify that there is a positive global trend of many national governments and public entities incorporating behavioral insights into their practices, including in Australia, Singapore, the Netherlands, Germany, and many other countries (Angawi & Hasanain, 2018).

As described in Section 2.2, a key early finding in this field was in the area of retirement savings behavior (Madrian & Shea, 2001). This finding ultimately led to the 2006 Pension Protection Act. Signed into law by President George W. Bush on August 17, 2006, this law made several provisions to protect retirement accounts, but it also made it significantly easier for employers to enroll their employees into 401(k) plans through an "autosave" feature (Beshears et al., 2010). Specifically, the Pension Protection Act encouraged employers to use automatic enrollment, where employees (after given notice) were automatically enrolled in their retirement accounts unless they explicitly chose not to participate. In addition, employers could make contributions to employee accounts (whether or not the employee chose to participate) or as a match. Finally, contribution rates could be automatically increased over time and those contributions could be defaulted into a diversified portfolio of assets. The Pension Protection Act had broad bipartisan support (it passed in the US Senate with a vote of 93–5 and a House of Representatives vote of 279–131). It was designed based on clear evidence and could be implemented in a fully transparent, nondeceptive manner. Other countries have since adopted similar legislation. To illustrate, the Parliament of the United Kingdom passed the Pensions Act of 2008, which stated that workers had to opt out of the pension plan offered by their employer – as opposed to opting in.[1]

After the ideas from *Nudge* spread, Cass Sunstein received an opportunity to put them into practice in the US federal government. The book *Simpler* (Sunstein, 2014) lays out many of the lessons learned after his appointment as administrator for the US Office of Information and Regulatory Affairs (OIRA) during President Barack Obama's first term. The OIRA was established as a part of the 1980 Paperwork Reduction Act and is housed within the Office of Management and Budget. Its primary function is to oversee the implementation of government-wide policies that pertain to information technology and privacy policy. Sunstein served from 2009 to 2012 and incorporated many insights from psychology and behavioral economics into this work. In *Simpler*, he maintains that the government can and should be streamlined to improve well-being, through solutions such as simplified administrative processes and improved communication of everyday information.

In 2010, the United Kingdom established the Behavioral Insights Team (BIT), which was also the first government-wide "nudge" unit in the world. The BIT was established within the UK cabinet office to explicitly apply insights from behavioral science across the government. Some of their most prominent work included using letters to increase the payment rate of a vehicle excise tax, nudging a higher rate of payment of fines by sending text messages,

---

[1] See the Pensions Act 2008, Statute Law Database, www.legislation.gov.uk/ukpga/2008/30/contents.

and using a lottery system to increase voter participation (John, 2014). The BIT was privatized and became a social purpose company in 2014; it now has a global reach – working not only with national governments but also with local authorities, nonprofits, and private entities alike.

Around the same time as the establishment of the BIT in the United Kingdom, a US federal agency was launching its own large-scale effort to explore the application of behavioral insights within its own programs. The Behavioral Interventions to Advance Self-Sufficiency (BIAS) project ran from 2010 to 2016. This work was sponsored by the Office of Planning, Research, and Evaluation in the Administration for Children and Families (ACF) at the US Department of Health and Human Services. This was the first effort by a US federal agency to apply and evaluate the use of behavioral insights in public policy design and implementation. The BIAS project applied behavioral science in the context of ACF-funded initiatives (namely, childcare and work support). Through a collaboration with local implementing agencies and a large team of academic scholars, BIAS tested 15 interventions with nearly 100,000 participants across 7 states (Richburg-Hayes et al., 2017). The BIAS findings included interventions that increased the use of quality childcare by low-income working families, increased frequency of both child support payments and requests for child support order modifications, and increased the rate of childcare subsidy renewals. The BIAS interventions used techniques such as novel communication (e.g., postcards) to prime and remind individuals of actions that they needed to take, designing and delivering assistance to ensure proper completion of complex paperwork, and using identity priming and social norms to increase the perceived desirability of specific actions. The ACF launched the BIAS – Next Generation project in 2015 to build on the success of the fifteen initial BIAS trials. This work has expanded the scope of the original endeavor to explore other areas, such as child welfare and head start programs and working with Temporary Assistance for Needy Families agencies on service delivery.

As the work of BIAS was underway, seeds were planted for an even larger effort within the federal government. The Social and Behavioral Sciences Team (SBST) was chaired by the White House Office of Science and Technology Policy (OSTP). The OSTP worked to explore the potential application of behavioral insights in the US government, and SBST was subsequently established by a 2015 executive order issued by President Barack Obama.[2] This is the

---

[2] See *Using Behavioral Science Insights to Better Serve the American People* – Executive Order No. 13,707 (September 15, 2015), Whitehouse.Gov, https://obamawhitehouse.archives.gov/the-press-office/2015/09/15/executive-order-using-behavioral-science-insights-better-serve-american.

executive order cited in the epigraph to this Element, and this effort was one of the most high-profile examples of the use of applied behavioral insights in the United States. Among many other projects, SBST used evidence-based elements in email communication to prompt student loan borrowers who were struggling to make payments to enter a loan rehabilitation agreement, and connected veterans with a range of social benefits such as career counseling, education, and health benefits (showing that improved email communication generally worked more effectively than other communication interventions such as letters or postcards). More broadly, they also provided guidance to the federal government on how to more efficiently and effectively engage with the individuals served by its policies and programs. The SBST extensively partnered with academics to create collaboration between behavioral scientists and federal agencies. These projects were outlined in detail in their annual reports and discussed in subsequent scholarly publications (Benartzi et al., 2017; Congdon & Shankar, 2015). It is worth emphasizing that these efforts have relied heavily on psychological theories and the application of those theories. As we proceed in this discussion, we will further explore why this underscores the need for scholars of social psychology, in particular, to continue to engage deeply and meaningfully in this work.

We should also note that in the United States this work has found a permanent home in the federal Office of Evaluation Sciences (OES).[3] Based at the General Services Administration, OES provides federal agencies with the technical expertise and guidance needed to establish evidence and use it in their decision-making. Much of this work incorporates behavioral insights, testing interventions in the field using randomized controlled trials. For example, a communication intervention in collaboration with the Department of Education increased the identification of students experiencing housing insecurity by 12 percent – 3.62 more students in each local education agency, on average (Shephard et al., 2020). The identification of these students subsequently enabled school staff to attempt to connect them with resources. In this study, the frequency, timing, content, and structure of the messages were carefully constructed, taking into account previous behavioral insights. For example, this intervention leveraged the knowledge that breaking down information into smaller chunks can improve processing (Wright et al., 2019) and that checklists can improve attention to important aspects of an information source (Emmons et al., 2018). These elements (among others) were included in the intervention, which was delivered to school staff in a series of periodic email communications.

---

[3] See the Office of Evaluation Sciences (OES) website: oes.gsa.gov.

Since its establishment in 2015, the team at OES has partnered with dozens of federal agencies and a team of experts from a diverse array of scholarly disciplines. This work has further expanded as President Joe Biden, in the early days of his administration, issued an executive action on building evidence in government.[4] In this memo, the president states a need to restore trust in the government by pursuing "scientific integrity and evidence-based policymaking."

We stress that influential scholarship in this field has not been limited to scholars and populations within the United States (some examples have already been discussed). On a global scale, the total number of public entities utilizing behavioral science has grown immensely in the past decade. As of 2018, the count was greater than 200. Drawing on data first reported in *Behavioural Insights and Public Policy: Lessons from around the World*, published by the Organisation for Economic Co-operation and Development (OECD, 2017), the supplemental figure has undergone a series of updates since its original publication, largely expanding the number of organizations included.[5] For example, Laboratorio de Gobierno (LabGob) – Chile's government innovation lab established in 2015 – has a declared prioritization of promoting public sector innovation through user-centered public management efforts. Scholars in the United Kingdom have explored strategies that rely on nudging individuals versus cultivating space for deep thought and debate (John et al., 2009). They directly describe how these approaches can prove beneficial for public policy challenges.

Other nations have brought together academics, industry, and local officials to promote behavioral insights in all areas of government – including environmental behavior, transportation, vaccinations, veterans' affairs, and education. And some nations credit their prosperity to the thoughtful integration of nudging and behavioral insights that promote the public good, as is the case for Singapore (Keating, 2018), which has documented success in public health and safety initiatives. Indeed, some powerful perspectives from outside of the United States directly examine combined approaches that go beyond simple nudges. The previously discussed article on nudging as an approach to public policy and governance was also led by a group of scholars outside of the United States (Mols et al., 2015). In addition, a recent edition of the World Bank's *World Development Report* explored the significance of the behavioral sciences

---

[4] See *Memorandum on Restoring Trust in Government Through Scientific Integrity and Evidence-Based Policymaking* (January 27, 2021), Whitehouse.Gov, www.whitehouse.gov/briefing-room/presidential-actions/2021/01/27/memorandum-on-restoring-trust-in-government-through-scientific-integrity-and-evidence-based-policymaking/.

[5] The supplemental figure is available at www.cambridge.org/publicpolicy.

in approaching issues faced by developing countries (World Bank, 2014). This perspective was critiqued for, among other issues, neglecting structural issues faced by these countries. The authors of this critique argued that a behavioral science approach to global health problems is reductionist and that the World Bank report fails to appropriately acknowledge this shortcoming (Fine et al., 2016). This dialogue speaks to the robust recent dialogue among scholars about the practical application of behavioral science in many contexts. Taken together, these individual events signal the massive shift in the way that governments around the world have viewed and appreciated the contributions of behavioral insights and psychology (see also Cialdini, 2018).

This section has provided evidence of the rapid rise and celebration of behavioral science (namely, psychology and behavioral economics) as a way to make governments more effective and efficient. These approaches to policy design, implementation, and evaluation continue to be explored by scholars, practitioners, and policymakers. For example, recent papers in the area of Public Management present an argument about nudging specifically for public policy and governance issues, and how governments use these tools for communication with their stakeholders (Esmark, 2019; Ewert, 2020). Next, we explore some examples of successes and challenges in the application of behavioral insights to public policy over the years.

3 Behavioral Insights: Successes and Shortcomings

While the majority of behavioral insights applications have produced small and limited effects, several examples of highly salient and publicized large impact, low-cost interventions have motivated the wide deployment of behavioral insights to public policy. Indeed, behavioral insights have proven successful in improving outcomes in a diverse set of policy areas, including environmental and health domains.

3.1 Interventions in Environment Policy

There has been much discussion of the role that behavioral science can play in the development and implementation of energy policy (Allcott & Mullainathan, 2010). Behavioral economics has often been used to create "paternalistic" policies to encourage energy efficiency (Allcott, 2016). The impacts of interventions in this space have been complex but compelling (Allcott & Rogers, 2014). The well-known Opower program provides an excellent case study.

Opower was a company founded by two Harvard University graduates with the goal of engaging utility customers in the understanding of their energy use. Their initial service involved the creation of highly detailed home-energy reports that relied on behavioral insights, with the goal of motivating individual households to lower their energy consumption. Opower provided feedback about homeowners' energy usage relative to other comparable homes in the community. This approach was based on prior research on social norms that demonstrated that descriptive normative messages were more likely to impact behavior. Moreover, to limit the likelihood that energy-efficient homes would use *more* rather than less energy, they found a way to avoid undesired "boomerang" effects using injunctive messaging that communicated societal approval or disapproval of homeowners' energy usage (Schultz et al., 2007). That study helped to unpack the previously mixed impacts of social norms interventions on behavior. The Opower study notably incorporated smiley face icons for those who used less energy than average in their neighborhood. Their reports caused initial action and, in several cases, showed persistent effects over a two-year period, while other cases showed attenuation over time (Allcott, 2011). This work provides a remarkable applied exploration of how injunctive and descriptive norms interact to impact real-world behavior. It is also informative to study the longer-term welfare effects of nudges in these spaces, to understand how they interact with traditional modes of evaluation (Allcott & Kessler, 2019). Doing so also enables the examination of boundary conditions – for example, 2019 results from OES showed that feedback about energy use (with comparisons to neighbors) did not decrease energy use by public housing residents (OES, 2019). Several social psychological theories can inform why this may be the case.

More broadly, a case can be made for the role of human behavior in the environmental challenges faced on our planet today. Many scholars and practitioners have attempted to nudge individuals into more environmentally friendly behavior. There has been some evidence for the use of insights such as behavioral influence on decision-making in areas such as meat consumption, transit choices, and water use. One large review of 160 interventions provides compelling evidence for where these approaches have been successful (Byerly et al., 2018). In this paper, they acknowledge the useful set of tools that behavioral science provides, discussing examples such as social norms, changing defaults, and public commitments that have contributed to interventions with demonstrated success in domains such as recycling and energy use (Abrahamse & Steg, 2013; Kirakozian, 2016; Osbaldiston & Schott, 2012; Sheeran et al., 2016). At the same time, they also acknowledge several key areas of opportunity that could deepen the implications of this work for public policy, such as a more focused exploration of interventions in domains that have the largest potential impacts on the environment (rather than testing the low-hanging fruit that may ultimately have a smaller global impact). These include holding large polluters (in the public and private sector) accountable to their outsized impact on the environment. Moreover, additional research highlights the ironic potential for behavioral insights interventions that nudge small-scale behaviors to crowd out – or substantively reduce – support for more comprehensive policy and regulation, in favor of quick fix, small-scale solutions (e.g., Hagmann et al., 2019).

3.2 Interventions in Health Policy

Behavioral insights have also found a prominent role in the domain of health and decision-making. Some of this work focuses on *avoiding* behaviors such as smoking (Dede, 2019). There has also been much work on encouraging positive behaviors such as consuming a healthy diet and engaging in regular exercise. One important study looked at nudges for guiding decision-making about diet (Arno & Thomas, 2016). This meta-analysis found an average increase of 15.3 percent in healthier choices, measured by frequency of "healthy" choices or overall consumption of calories. The study contexts analyzed here ranged from laboratory studies on consumption to field studies in contexts such as movie theaters and cafeterias. The interventions also ranged widely, from simple nudges on portion size (or presentation of calorie-count information) to observations of social effects (e.g., observing amount consumed when eating alone versus with peers). Other researchers have studied nudging to increase selection of fruits and vegetables specifically. One meta-analysis found that many of these interventions have a moderate effect and that changing placement (and other combined approaches) have the largest impacts on behavior (Broers et al., 2017). Another found that interventions are relatively more effective at *reducing* unhealthy eating rather than increasing healthful eating (or reducing total consumption) – providing an even more nuanced potential understanding of these efforts (Cadario & Chandon, 2019).

Of critical note, much of the above work was done in the United States, and the remainder in similarly wealthy nations. While there have been many examples of "success" of these nudges, Arno and Thomas (2016) underscore the need to understand these impacts in more diverse contexts. There is far less evidence on the extent to which these types of health interventions are successful in contexts outside of the wealthy, Western world. Moreover, there is a gap in understanding the effectiveness of these interventions among subpopulations *within* countries (of all socioeconomic standings). There have been few studies specifically exploring health policy nudges in low-income and minority populations. Some evidence suggests that these interventions may work in these contexts as well. In one study, a simple color-coding system in a cafeteria encouraging the choice of healthier foods (labeled green) over less healthy foods (labeled red) was successful (Levy et al., 2012). However, other scholars have argued that more traditional financial subsidies are necessary to create sustained behavior change in communities with less access to healthy and fresh food (Hebda & Wagner, 2016). Broadly, there is not substantial evidence as to whether or not these findings hold up when examining, for example, low-income populations or communities of color, and there is much opportunity to more deeply explore these questions, with a focus on how these approaches operate among diverse populations. This is a theme and issue that we will engage at length later in this Element.

Furthermore, recent work has argued that often nudges do not replicate because many researchers take a "kitchen sink" approach, simultaneously applying many previously successful elements of various nudges to a given problem. When there are several components of an intervention working at the same time, it becomes impossible to tease out, specifically, which was most effective. A more nuanced attempt to understand the target population can help to "budge" individuals from their existing belief structures (Hauser et al., 2018). This approach could inform a better understanding of the conditions under which elements of interventions are effective for generating behavior change and for whom. The next section provides further evidence of settings in which behavioral insights have been applied without producing the intended effects.

3.3 Shortcomings of Behavioral Insights

While there has been much to celebrate, additional evidence has demonstrated that relatively low-cost behavioral approaches and nudges to large and complex social problems do not always work as intended. For example, some prominent scholars have explored the question of whether (and how much) governments ought to invest time and effort in nudging (Benartzi et al., 2017). In this paper, the authors argue that nudging can often be a cost-effective way of improving well-being (when combined with traditional incentives and interventions). They compare the costs and effectiveness of multiple interventions across several domains and document consistently cost-effective, yet significant, findings relative to other economic and traditional interventions. However, they note that more research must continue to be done in this space to understand the impacts of nudging. Because of publication bias, the extent to which any particular approach works or does not work can be difficult to discern. Most of the time, the scholarly community is only exposed to the successes. However, the rise of preregistration is starting to change these patterns.

This is particularly important for nudges that are intended to inform public policy design and implementation. For example, groups like OES make a point of publishing preregistration, analysis plans, and final abstracts for every study conducted, even for those that reveal null or otherwise unexpected results. These practices illuminate the importance of recognizing the boundaries and contexts under which behavioral insights effects are reliable or minimal. An increasing culture of transparency in psychology not only will address scientific practices that tend to increase the likelihood of identifying an effect in a situation where none truly exists (Simmons et al., 2011) but may also increase our understanding of exactly under what conditions psychological effects are robust. From a policy perspective, this approach is critical. It would be irresponsible to spend time and other resources attempting to test and subsequently scale up findings that are fickle and difficult to replicate, both inside and outside of the lab. In the following sections, we unpack more of the systematic ways that behavioral insights have not lived up to their promise.

3.4 Additional Considerations in the Context of Public Policy

Failures of nudging go beyond the observation of null effects. Thaler and Sunstein have also described the issue of "sludge." Sludge encompasses frictions and barriers that make it more difficult for people to do what they intend to do. These are often interventions and activities that are "nudging for evil" (Thaler, 2018, p. 201). This can make it even harder to achieve widespread public good and prosocial behavior (Sunstein, 2021). Importantly, there are productive forms of sludge as well, such as waiting periods following gun purchasing, that aim to promote public welfare and safety. Therein lies the challenge of thoughtful and contextual application of behavioral insights to public policy – where administrative burden is both detrimental and beneficial depending on context. Observing sludges and nudges provides additional evidence for why transparency in public policy is of key importance (Mills, 2020). One prominent example of this was a Supreme Court ruling that allowed Ohio to purge voters who had not voted in several elections and failed to respond to notices from election officials.[6] These "dark nudges" have also been documented in the alcohol industry: information often normalizes and encourages alcohol consumption, while minimizing the emphasis on its potential harms. Ultimately, this has the potential to result in misinformation (Petticrew et al., 2020).

---

[6] See *Husted* v. *A. Phillip Randolph Institute* (United States Supreme Court June 11, 2018), www.supremecourt.gov/opinions/17pdf/16-980_f2q3.pdf.

Cass Sunstein (2020) has proposed "sludge audits" as one way to cope with this problem. This (admittedly time- and resource-intensive) process would require both the public and the private sector to examine their systems, practices, and processes for sludge, measure the costs and impacts thereof, and decide when and how to manage or reduce it. From a public policy perspective, this is especially important when the individuals being significantly impacted are members of vulnerable populations. Others have argued that alternatives to nudging should be preferable. For example, Gigerenzer makes the case that some nudges focus on individual shortcomings rather than larger external factors (such as substantial resources spent by corporations to influence behavior). Another alternative might be to provide opportunities for individuals to improve their understanding of risk and other decision elements (Gigerenzer, 2015). At any rate, a technique such as Sunstein proposes warrants a place in this literature, as it will allow for deeper understanding of the contextual features present in complex decision environments – especially those relevant to improving the public good.

We are not the first scholars to suggest that the field of applied behavior science must revisit the psychological roots of nudging approaches (Marchiori et al., 2017; Mols et al., 2015); our work expands on the themes of such arguments. We contend that a better understanding of the conditions (and boundaries) of nudging is critical to the long-term and increased success of this approach. More importantly, this approach will allow for deeper and more authentic considerations of equity – in addition to efficiency and efficacy – in this space, which has to date been largely absent. There is ample opportunity to consider different predictors of behavior. One recent paper (in the domain of consumer behavior) shows that the predictors of consumption at the individual level (values, attitudes, income, and education) are distinct from those that operate at the country level (national wealth, post-materialist values) (Milfont & Markowitz, 2016). This type of exploration provides for a much more nuanced consideration of the boundary conditions and policy implications of these approaches in different domains. These approaches are particularly important for considering the way that scholars and practitioners can continue to partner together to change health behaviors, as has been increasingly acknowledged by the field of public administration more broadly (Vlaev et al., 2016).

3.5 The Present Argument

Behavioral insights have certainly provided an innovative approach to the design and implementation of public policy. However, there is a significant (often unspoken) problem: effect sizes are notoriously small (Cohen's d coefficient between 0.10 and 0.29; Cohen, 1988), suggesting weak, potentially unstable relationships between nudging interventions and measured outcomes, and predominate in the (relatively young) world of applied behavioral insights – though we do concede that defaults seem to present an exception to this pattern (see Hummel & Maedche, 2019). This critique of small effect sizes is present in the broader field of psychology (Hemphill, 2003; Richard et al., 2003). Benartzi and colleagues (2017), discussing nudging in governments, hint at this problem. And indeed, some of the significant and effective implementations of nudges to public domains are the exception rather than the rule, with many other efforts and initiatives showing limited to no behavior change (see DellaVigna & Linos, 2022). This has become increasingly clear given the mandatory reporting of behavioral insights interventions undergone by governments (e.g., OES and BIT). Often, nudges (and similar behavioral interventions) are based on psychological effects that are subtle, and thus often unstable, when explored in the incredibly complex real world. Researchers must acknowledge these problems in the design of their research. This includes both applied researchers – those implementing behavioral insights in varying contexts – and basic scholars who, regardless of their interests in the application of the work, must acknowledge where their findings have boundary conditions and generalizability constraints. Public policy needs deliberate efforts to understand these factors, instead of the implicit and unspoken assumption that a small net benefit at the aggregate level is good enough. In the long run, a singular focus on smaller nudges will not serve the broader good – we explore this idea in depth in Section 4. Indeed, this runs parallel with recent compelling arguments that the psychological sciences must develop and augment cumulative theoretical frameworks for developing and testing hypotheses across diverse contexts, in an effort to develop theories of human behavior (Muthukrishna & Henrich, 2019). Researchers have a responsibility to design and implement research that allows both academic and nonacademic scholars to understand the factors that will matter in practice (such as personality, demographics, context, and culture).

Ultimately, this is a crucial equity issue. Without considering the nuance of and complex effects within nudging, the field has the potential to exacerbate existing disparities with respect to many crucial outcomes. In addition, the continued prioritization of efficiency and cost-effectiveness will undermine the potential to identify more sustainable behavior change efforts that account for the richness of the people whose behavior is being impacted. In the following pages, we argue that social psychology has some of the key tools necessary to unpack and improve the design and implementation of efforts to use behavioral science in these applied settings and should do so with equity as a guiding principle.

4 A Constrained Context: Concerns and Challenges for Applying Behavioral Sciences

Thus far we have outlined examples of both successful and less fruitful efforts to nudge and influence individual and collective behavior toward promoting desirable social outcomes. By and large, there have been a number of compelling examples in which researchers and policymakers have either nudged or subtly guided individuals to save for retirement, cut down their utility usage, engage in healthful behavior, and recycle more, as well as numerous other prosocial behaviors. Importantly, we propose that the practices and research processes that enabled us to learn a great deal about human behavior, while instrumental, are not sufficient for moving forward our examination of how individuals navigate the social world. In particular, current efforts around research questions, experimental design, and data analyses limit the ability of psychologists to clarify and uncover the many nuanced, yet foundational, considerations needed to better understand whether efforts to shift people's behavior in applied contexts are experienced equitably – both in their benefits and in their challenges and risks.

As noted in Section 3, when assessing whether a behavioral insight intervention has been effective, much of the social psychological research emphasizes the elicited behavioral intentions or behavior. Nudges that elicit the hypothesized behavior are deemed successful and those that elicit no behavior change or counter-behavior (e.g., reactance) are considered failed interventions. On the surface, this approach seems logical and is common practice in the field. However, we contend that a great deal is missing from this process – in particular, the emphasis on whether a desired behavior has been elicited or not over an aggregate population as indication of a successful application of behavioral insights fails to surface a number of additional considerations. Consistent with this notion, the OECD's *Tools and Ethics for Applied Behavioural Insights: The Basic Toolkit* identifies several important ethical considerations surrounding the implementation of behavioral insights to applied contexts. They include "Are there any potential risks or unintended consequences when pursuing the desired behavior?" and "Are there uneven risks (i.e., positive for the majority but harmful risks for minority groups)?" (OECD, 2019, p. 21). Despite social psychology's emphasis on examining the interaction of the person with environment and context, these questions have not been substantively engaged in research to date. From a policy perspective, this is a significant shortcoming, but it is also one that could be addressed with more thoughtful engagement in the design and evaluation of research approaches.

In what follows, we take up and advance the call for a more nuanced consideration, identification, and application of behavioral insights in applied contexts. Moreover, we contend that basic and applied social psychology has the tools to answer this call. Applied domains, including public policy, draw extensively from basic and applied social psychological research to inform practices and processes. These domains include numerous stakeholders: governments, nonprofits, think tanks, public sector consultants, and the private sector. To date, these domains have been both informed and constrained by the research generated in social psychology for guiding intervention design and other behavior change efforts. Thus, what limitations and challenges are present in social psychological research get transferred and amplified at an increased scale in these applied domains. For this reason, we contend that social psychology, as both a basic and an applied discipline, has to answer the call of generating a more nuanced science to better serve the application of this science for key stakeholders.

In this section, we consider two key insights. First, we delve into the psychological consequences, in addition to behavioral outcomes, for the adaptation of behavioral insights to applied domains. In particular, we provide evidence of the often overlooked considerations of stigmatization and emotional taxes that can result from behavioral insight interventions. Second, we examine evidence that challenges and benefits of behavioral insights may not be evenly distributed across the population, creating disadvantages for those who are already worse off. We focus on outcomes across several domains in which promoting individual well-being has both personal and collective benefits. Across both of these critical areas of consideration, we center equity in our examination.

4.1 WEIRD Participants and Researchers

In considering the ability for social psychology to substantively and ethically inform applied behavioral insights domains, we must first consider the discipline's research practices and processes. Doing so enables us to consider unexamined elements that foster inequitable examination and application of behavioral insights. Social psychology values universalism. Indeed, one prominent goal of the discipline is an emphasis on considering whether or not there are basic and foundational human behaviors and psychological processes that transcend contexts and people. But our current practices limit the field's ability to draw universal conclusions and translate these to applied domains. Over recent decades, researchers have underscored a WEIRD prevalence in social psychology (Ceci et al., 2010; Henrich et al., 2010). The tendency to over-emphasize the role of Western, educated, industrialized, rich, and democratic contexts and psychologies has proliferated in social psychology, and psychology more broadly. In 2008, Arnett documented that between 2003 and 2007, 68 percent of studies published in the six top APA journals relied on samples from the United States, and some 96 percent relied on samples from Western and industrialized nations (i.e., Europe, Australia, Israel, and North American) (Arnett, 2008). The original 2008 piece was reprinted in 2016, underscoring the severity of this problem. Examining social psychology in particular, the *Journal of Personality and Social Psychology*, social psychology's flagship journal, also suffers from this problem. Henrich and colleagues have argued that the social psychological community should be the most attentive to questions of participant backgrounds and contexts (Henrich et al., 2010), and yet 62 percent of the samples in this journal were North American (94 percent when examining Western and industrialized nations), and of these samples, 67 percent were undergraduates from psychology courses.

These patterns are even more striking when considered at the global scale. Eighty-three percent of US samples in the *Journal of Personality and Social Psychology* were majority Caucasian (Arnett, 2008) and similar findings have been documented in other examinations of the field (S. O. Roberts et al., 2020), leading some scholars to contend that "Western" could reliably be replaced with "White" when examining WEIRD populations in psychological research (Dupree & Kraus, 2022; Nzinga et al., 2018). Importantly, we do not contend that Western samples are monolithic. There is a great deal of diversity and difference among these samples and we will address this more substantively in Section 4.2. Nevertheless, there are considerable concerns that stem from this overrepresentation of certain nations and samples. WEIRD populations are not merely unrepresentative samples but markedly so (Henrich et al., 2010). Arnett (2008) poignantly asks "Is a focus on 5% of the world's population sufficient for portraying the psychological functioning of the human species?" We contend that it is not, and even less so when we consider that this psychology then informs public policy and administration decisions as well as other domains. There are emerging perspectives on how to make sense of the cultural differences between populations, and these are crucial steps to mitigating the effects of the significant WEIRD prevalence in the field (e.g., Muthukrishna et al., 2020).

In addition to highlighting the extensive underrepresentation of non-Western contexts in social psychological research, it is of note that much of our science –

research question development, hypothesis testing, data analysis, and reporting of results – is done by researchers from WEIRD contexts. Indeed, first authors on APA manuscripts are overwhelmingly – 96 percent – from US, European, and other English-speaking countries (Arnett, 2008). Given that the APA is a North American society, this finding may not be all that surprising, but given the high degree of influence and power this society has in the broader field of social psychology, it is worth consideration. And others have highlighted that most cultural psychology researchers are White males from the United States, which is an example of a culture, but one that is disproportionately represented in the global space. In addition to a lack of representation of non-Western perspectives in the scholarly community, there is much evidence that our research practices center WEIRD populations in the design of our research questions.

4.2 WEIRD research practices

When considering the findings that many participants as well as researchers are drawn from nonrepresentative populations, an additional consideration becomes clear: much of social psychology is well-tailored to designing experiments for and exploring the psychological processes of WEIRD populations. Despite examining how the real or imagined presence of others shapes and biases people's behavior, social psychologists are also human and, as such, have the potential to be unaware of our own blind spots when developing research (Dupree & Kraus, 2022; Nzinga et al., 2018; Rad et al., 2018). That is, the questions that researchers explore are often framed by the social context in which those researchers are raised and trained and their participants are found, and to the extent that WEIRD contexts are overrepresented, it increases the likelihood that these circumscribed contexts will be overrepresented in the findings. That is, when developing research protocols, stimuli are more likely to be designed with WEIRD populations in mind – in the selection of cultural references, choice of language, pacing, and presentation. These protocols are also more likely to be well-suited to test hypotheses developed and refined by WEIRD researchers that emphasize examining phenomena in WEIRD environments with dependence on data from WEIRD populations. These findings are then highlighted by social and political elites and, subsequently, deployed in public policy efforts.

Importantly, given the field's tendency and preference to seek out universal behaviors, there is the potential to overgeneralize the research findings – drawing conclusions that lack cultural and sociodemographic nuance. Rozin noted the limited demographic information provided about participant race, social class, religiosity, or the time point in history that data are collected (Rozin, 2001). Consistent with this finding, DeJesus and colleagues note that, of the nearly 1,150 articles published in 11 psychology journals between 2015 and 2016, the majority of articles failed to mention the race (73 percent) or socioeconomic status (79 percent) of research participants (DeJesus et al., 2019). A more localized examination by Rad and colleagues notes that, in 2014, 72 percent of abstracts published in *Psychological Science* did not mention participant race, 83 percent did not report analyses of any effects of sample diversity, and 84 percent omitted cultural context considerations (Rad et al., 2018). And this concern persists, with similar results found in an analysis of *Psychological Science* publications from 2017. Perhaps most striking, 84 percent of published articles do not even take the relatively small step of recommending the possibility of examining the findings across cultural contexts (Rad et al., 2018).

Taken together, psychology, and social psychology in particular, has a relative strength in the ability to understand and shift behavior and psychological processes among general WEIRD populations. However, the field has a relative weakness in its ability to examine differential outcomes both within WEIRD populations and outside of them. The limited integration and examination of sociodemographic characteristics among research drawn from WEIRD samples and the dearth of representation from much of the world's population limit this possibility. Moreover, the preference for brevity of language (DeJesus et al., 2019) and desirability of universalist and generalizable claims (Rad et al., 2018) stifle our examination of disaggregated data. From an applied behavioral science perspective, the consequences have the potential to be significant. As public policy and other applied domains adopt and adapt the findings from social psychology at scale, they often do so without realizing the limited scope in which the data were collected – after all, this information is rarely provided in publications. This potentially increases the likelihood that large-scale interventions will be designed in a manner that reflects and reinforces WEIRD perspectives and decision-making. Thus, there is a strong and concerning potential for misalignment between basic and applied social psychological research and behavioral insights applications in other domains. Indeed, if we start to clarify and disaggregate the data, we are likely to get a different (better and more nuanced) understanding of how the application of behavioral insights shape behavior and psychology.

4.3 Underexamined Psychological Taxes

Largely missing from this discussion is a more nuanced consideration of the psychological impacts of behavioral interventions. Social psychology as a field has extensively considered human psychology in examining and shaping how individuals make decisions and how changes to context and mindset shape those decisions. Critically, this same consideration has not been given due diligence in understanding the *impact* of behavioral interventions – particularly, the psychological costs of stigma, negative emotion activation, and their impact on cognitive depletion. There is a significant opportunity to recenter social psychology's contributions to behavioral insights interventions by incorporating psychological outcomes alongside behavioral ones. Indeed, failing to consider both the behavioral and the psychological impact of nudges and behavioral interventions limits the efficacy and sustainability of such behavior change efforts.

Consideration of the psychological impact of behavioral interventions is key given the reliance of nudges on social norms and the real or imagined presence of others in the environment. This is particularly the case for nudges that stigmatize or "otherize" undesirable behaviors and, as a consequence, the individuals who engage in these behaviors. Scholars have articulated that efforts centered around nudging and behavioral insights applications impose an emotional tax on individuals (Glaeser, 2005; Loewenstein & O'Donoghue, 2006). For example, public health campaigns that aim to educate on smoking and safe sex behaviors (Glaeser, 2005) or obesity (Loewenstein & O'Donoghue, 2006) aim to make behaviors related to these activities seem dangerous and unenjoyable. Doing so has the potential to activate both self-stigmatization processes and societal stigmatization that devalues members of subgroups engaging in the devalued behavior, especially because individuals may not consciously process the intent to nudge their behavior.

The use of stigma as a behavior change tool has received both critique and support from scholars. Some have noted that a slight degree of shame and stigma experienced at the individual level can be a motivating force for behavior change (Eyal, 2014). In some cases, these approaches can promote public welfare and the aggregate good, and thus are deemed worthy efforts. For example, while efforts to stigmatize smoking may result in interpersonal and social costs that make smokers' lives more challenging, the aggregate social welfare of reducing cigarette smoking may justify the implementation of effective minimal stigma-inducing behavior change efforts (Eyal, 2014). Other scholars have offered an alternative view, one that centers the psychological experience of stigma, noting that shame is quite psychologically potent and has the potential to elicit stronger emotional reactions, such as heightened anger (Tieffenbach, 2014).

Moreover, the self-stigmatization that may result from nudges has been underexamined. Self-stigmatization, which includes internalization of negative stereotypes of devalued behaviors, can negatively impact an individual's well-being and sense of self-worth (Bos et al., 2013). It can motivate patterns of behavior that aim to conceal stigmatized attributes, activating increased stress and anxiety in the process. Scholars have noted that individuals who hold certain stigmatizing traits interpret messages to change their behaviors distinctly from those who do not hold these attributes and dissect these messages to make inferences about the extent to which their characteristics will be devalued (Harmeling et al., 2021). Doing so shapes (decreased) interest in programs and efforts aimed at alleviating the stigma (Harmeling et al., 2021). These individual efforts scale up to consider more public and social devaluation of groups.

While some might argue that the broader societal devaluation of behavioral deviants is acceptable, it is worth noting that public permission to stigmatize individuals based on behaviors that are variably controllable and informed by multiple individual, interpersonal, and systemic factors is a slippery slope. It centers the individual as the change agent without considering the complex web of factors that shape that behavior – a key consideration in the policy world. Indeed, many scholars have noted the importance of structural stigma (see Bos et al., 2013; Corrigan & Lam, 2007), which are the "societal-level conditions, cultural norms, and institutional policies that constrain the opportunities, resources, and wellbeing of the stigmatized" (Hatzenbuehler & Link, 2014, p. 2). This is a central consideration for the application of behavioral insights to public policy. Moreover, while some might assess that a slight degree of public or interpersonal embarrassment is acceptable, calibrating that low grade of negative affect poses a challenge. As one paper notes, for shame to be an effective behavioral intervention strategy, researchers and practitioners must create a context in which slight embarrassment is more likely the outcome than a more significant (acute guilt and shame) emotional response as the latter may undermine behavior change efforts (Tieffenbach, 2014). Anticipating that one can calibrate on the appropriate level of stigma to be effective and do so across a population, as is often the case in applied behavioral science, is optimistic.

Critically, much of the behavioral science literature has not emphasized the individual, interpersonal, or societal psychological costs of behavioral interventions and nudges as they relate to stigma. In almost all instances, the "participants" in nudging interventions are not aware of these tactics. This underscores the need for scholars to actively consider and measure the psychological and societal costs that are inadvertently created by these approaches. What limited research has examined these costs underscores the need for more nuanced data collection and research practices.

In the domain of curbing cigarette smoking behavior, recent research highlights the behavioral costs of stigma. Numerous public health and service efforts often develop media messaging aimed at reducing smoking behavior that focuses on the personal and collective health costs. Negative messages have been central to many of these campaigns, including efforts to redesign cigarette packaging with graphic images of the health consequences of smoking (Fong et al., 2009; Wakefield et al., 2013). Such efforts aim to reduce undesirable behavior by inducing fear, guilt, and shame for engaging in said behavior and there is some evidence of their effectiveness for behavioral intentions to reduce smoking (Wakefield et al., 2013). Importantly, recent work highlights that these messages can induce stereotype threat – concerns that one will be judged through a negative lens or confirm negative stereotypes about an identity group that is of personal relevance. Among a community sample of smokers, those exposed to stigmatizing public health messages aimed at reducing smoking were less able to delay smoking their first cigarette compared to participants in the control condition (Cortland et al., 2019). Others document that stigmatization leads individuals who see smoking as an important part of their self-concept to experience emotional and cognitive depletion and discount the negative impacts of smoking on their own health (Helweg-Larsen et al., 2019). Importantly, these effects varied by population, with significantly stronger effects of stigmatization on US participants, relative to diminished or absent effects for Danish participants. Given that smoking behavior is a coping strategy for anxiety and stress for some individuals, messages that stigmatize the behavior – thereby inducing anxiety – may have the ironic behavioral effect of promoting the undesired behavior in order to manage anxiety. At the aggregate level, such campaigns may serve to ostracize smokers from the broader population while also promoting the undesirable behavior among the stigmatized subgroup.

Psychological costs ought to also be a central consideration across behavioral insights applications. These same stigmatization patterns can be examined in efforts aimed at reducing obesity, which include calorie-salience nudges. Calorie-salience interventions aim to increase awareness of calories in various foods and, as a result, nudge individuals toward lower calorie food options. Thunström examined the emotional costs of just such a salience nudge. Participants were exposed to calorie information in a hypothetical social situation and then asked to select between meals that varied in caloric content (relatively high vs. low calories). While overall participants had an average positive reaction to the calorie-salience nudge, this effect was not experienced equally. In particular, negative emotional reactions were more prevalent among participants who had low eating self-control. That is, individuals who would be the intended targets and welfare beneficiaries of a calorie-salience nudge aimed at promoting lower calorie food consumption were most likely to report feeling negatively about the nudge – that is, they are emotionally taxed. In contrast, individuals with relatively high eating self-control – those already more able to control their caloric intake – were more likely to report positive affect toward the calorie-salience nudge (Thunström, 2019). This finding is consistent with work examining the stigma associated with weight and eating behavior, which documents that messages and signals that increase perceived weight stigma lead individuals who self-perceive as overweight to consume *more* calories and feel less in control of their eating behavior relative to individuals who do not perceive themselves as overweight (Major et al., 2014). In addition, social psychological research highlights the importance of removing stigma from applied behavioral contexts for promoting public welfare. For example, Hall and colleagues document that self-affirmation (a theory that suggests that people are strongly motivated to maintain their sense of self-worth and integrity) can mitigate the negative stigma associated with experiencing poverty. The self-affirmation activity, recalling a moment of feeling successful or proud, appeared to minimize the cognitive depletion associated with the stigmatizing effects of poverty (Hall et al., 2014). Indeed, the self-affirmation intervention, in addition to increasing executive control and fluid intelligence, resulted in participants seeking out public welfare resources that they were eligible for at higher rates than those who did not receive the same intervention.

Taken together, numerous behavioral nudge factors can elicit stigma, underscoring the importance of assessing psychological costs and outcomes as primary outcome considerations in behavioral insights. As noted earlier in this section, the experience of stigma may vary from mild to more significant and there is the potential for reactions to vary as a function of individual characteristics (Helweg-Larsen et al., 2019; Thunström, 2019) and broader cultural considerations (Krendl & Pescosolido, 2020).

A key contribution of social psychology to the broader domain of behavioral insights is the field's emphasis on examining outcomes and phenomena outside of economic and financial decisions. While behavioral economics centers on the impact of psychological processes for financial and economic decision-making, social psychology considers the questions of prosocial behavior, volunteering, intergroup processes, and social identity, to name a few. We are concerned with all aspects of what it means to be a social person interacting with the world around them. Thus, social psychology is well poised to recenter human psychology in the applications of behavioral insights, particularly emphasizing the potential psychological costs and taxes associated with behavior change interventions. In the applied context, recognizing and accounting for the psychological consequences of behavioral insights is critical to their sustainable implementation. There may be hesitancy to engage in this practice given the legitimate concern that self-report data is constrained by what individuals can articulate, verbalize, or express, and as such has been critiqued as less reliable (Haeffel & Howard, 2010; Nisbett & Wilson, 1977). However, this is not the case across all self-report assessments (e.g., Axt, 2018), and the ability to triangulate around the psychological experience of a behavioral intervention (e.g., identifying affective reactions to nudges) is a challenge psychologists can and must meet. To the extent that basic and applied social psychology fails to center the psychological experiences of behavioral interventions, we limit our ability to develop behavioral interventions that benefit those most marginalized and historically underrepresented in other domains, including public policy decisions.

4.4 Who Is Being Nudged

One key consideration from the limited examination of intersectional identity and cultural contexts in basic and applied social psychology is an oversimplification of intervention outcomes. As noted in Section 1, interventions that have an aggregate positive effect toward a desired behavior are considered helpful, and those that have an aggregate neutral or negative (i.e., reactance) behavior are deemed ineffective. Largely missing from the behavioral insights literature research is the question of effective or ineffective for *whom*.

In recent years, there has been an increasing call to examine psychology, including basic and applied social psychology, through an intersectional (Shih & Sanchez, 2009; Syed et al., 2018) and cultural lens (Brady et al., 2018). As noted in Section 4.3, these perspectives and lenses are largely absent in the literature. We contend that the consequences of this are particularly heightened for social psychology. Research from social psychology, given the field's emphasis on how individuals behave and make decisions and how these decisions are shaped by the environment and others, has impacts well beyond basic psychology and its subdisciplines. It is adapted to consultants, policymakers, and nonprofits ranging from local communities to ocean governance. These applications by and large engage communities and constituents far beyond the WEIRD individuals that make up much of the data. Scholars have argued that it is insufficient to know that distributional effects exist without also examining for whom and under what circumstances (Sunstein, 2014) and that governments have an ethical responsibility to consider distributional effects of behavioral insights (J. L. Roberts, 2018). To date, these effects are largely undocumented in published work. For the field to have sustained and equitable impact, we need better understanding of our data.

Research that has examined disaggregated effects underscores the importance of this call to broaden participation and increase the contextualization of psychological research. Indeed, recent work examining nudges aimed at improving welfare by promoting responsible spending behavior found that the effects of such public policy intervention tools are not distributed equally. In particular, efforts to curb spending and consumption behavior were particularly effective for those who already conserve their spending – deemed "tightwads" – leading these individuals who are less likely to spend money to spend even less. In contrast, for individuals who spend more liberally and would benefit from such an intervention – "spendthrifts" – the nudge did not significantly affect their spending behavior (Thunström et al., 2018). Thus, there is a distributional effect that favors those already engaging in welfare-promoting behavior, perhaps nudging them to their own detriment of not spending on well-being needs, and no effect on individuals who would benefit more from the nudge.

Returning to an earlier example, research similarly finds distributional effects among calorie-salience nudges aimed at curbing calorie consumption. In the aggregate, one study finds a positive welfare effect of calorie-salience nudges aimed at curbing consumption of high-calorie foods, suggesting a potentially useful tool (Thunström, 2019). However, the researcher's closer, disaggregated examination of the data suggests a more nuanced conclusion. The calorie-salience nudge was particularly effective for individuals who were already mindful of their eating behavior and had higher self-control in the domain of calorie consumption, leading them to further reduce their intended caloric intake (Thunström, 2019). However, this same nudge had a minimal positive or neutral behavioral effect on individuals with less self-control around their calorie consumption. Thus, the nudge was particularly effective for those less likely to require such a nudge – that is, those who already had a higher degree of self-control – and not those who were the intended beneficiaries, who as noted, also experienced more negative emotional reactions.

In the domain of energy usage, recent work highlights the distributional effects of choice default nudges (Ghesla et al., 2020). In particular, the researchers examined choice preferences for electricity contracts that ranged from less environmentally friendly and cheaper to more environmentally friendly and expensive. Absent a choice being made, residents were defaulted into a mid-tier choice on environmental friendliness and cost. Over a four-year period, residents in a small community were given the option to change their contract by contacting the electricity company. The scholars also conducted a survey assessing resident contract preferences absent a default option and contrasted this with the current resident plans. In aggregate, they found that having a default mid-tier option resulted in more environmentally friendly contracts relative to the preferences of residents absent a default. Importantly, by disaggregating the data they find that the presence of a default leads lower-income families to pay more for electricity than they would want to and there is a greater willingness by higher-income families to pay more than their current contracts. They note that, for the former, lower-income group, the default option acts as a hidden tax requiring greater payment than residents would actively choose. For the latter, there is an opportunity to promote greener contract selection over the default. Thus, while there are aggregate benefits of defaults in this context, the felt costs are not distributed equally. Moreover, work by Mrkva and colleagues further underscores the importance of examining distributional effects, particularly as they relate to defaults. They find that nudges that are well designed to benefit low socioeconomic status individuals result in positive benefits; in contrast, nudges that are not mindful of such considerations exacerbate disparities as lower socioeconomic status individuals are more likely to stick with the default (Mrkva et al., 2021), which has the potential to be less optimal.

Similar distributional effects of disparate impact on groups that are relatively worse off and whose welfare would benefit more from effective nudges have been documented in education interventions to increase student achievement. Work by Stephens and colleagues (2012) documents the distributional effects of education interventions for academic performance along social class categories. In one set of experiments, undergraduates from first-generation or continuing-generation educational backgrounds were exposed to messaging around university culture that emphasized either an interdependent (i.e., community-focused success) or an independent (i.e., individual path and success) environment. Experiment-based findings highlighted that first-generation college students felt a misalignment of their personal cultural values (situated in interdependence) compared to university cultural values (which were perceived to emphasize broad US norms of independence). First-generation college students exposed to messages that reified this perception consequently found academic tasks more difficult and performed worse compared to when these cultural values of interdependence were brought into alignment. This is of consequence given the broader university context as one that underscores independent cultural values and broad behavioral interventions aiming to promote college application and enrollment that may be particularly effective for continuing-generation individuals, who are more likely to see a cultural alignment, rather than first-generation students. Relatedly, efforts to promote student achievement via nudges aiming to improve study practices document benefits to students who are predisposed to study but not to lesser achieving students, who would arguably benefit to a greater degree from such interventions

(Auferoth, 2020). Together, this work raises the important consideration of nuance within WEIRD populations – these data were collected at an elite institution and yet they reflect significant effects of subdominant cultural variability, highlighting that even within WEIRD samples there is need and reason to examine disaggregated outcomes. Thus, education offers another meaningful example of the importance of considering distributional effects.

In considering the application of social psychology to behavior and decision-making, the field and researchers ought to emphasize interventions that benefit those who are the most negatively impacted. As we have explored here, this is even further supported by the idea that some behavioral insights may be experienced as subtle nudges for a subset of the population and as sludges for another subset. As Sunstein (2020) discusses, the negative impacts of excessive (and often unjustified) administrative frictions go beyond simple frustration and wasted time. These processes may also exacerbate the impacts of existing social stigma, create humiliation, and ultimately deprive vulnerable individuals of services and opportunities that they desperately need. It should be the responsibility of institutions to understand (and mitigate) the volume of sludge that decision makers encounter. Researchers can also consider the existence of these friction factors in the design and implementation of our interventions and field experiments.

Of particular note in the research summarized here is the finding that people who are relatively worse off are bearing the brunt of neutral and negative behavioral science outcomes and, absent the disaggregation of the data, these effects would not be illuminated. In each example noted in this section, there is an aggregate positive benefit of the nudge, which largely obscures negative welfare outcomes for "worse-off" groups. Thus, if social psychological research remains agnostic to sociodemographic and cultural considerations, the lack of disaggregated and distributional effects in our interventions has the potential to miss or cause harm to vulnerable populations. Importantly, we offer that a shift in how we do our science is needed to better understand these two considerations. This shift starts with better data for a more equitable science.

5 Better Data for Equitable Outcomes

Thus far we have provided an overview of the origins and implementations of behavioral insights in applied contexts. In addition, we have documented the successes and challenges in translating basic social psychological research to applied contexts of social psychological processes. In particular, the arguments have noted that applications of behavioral science are drawn from constrained contexts, which often do not consider the psychological impact of such efforts nor disaggregated and distributional effects. In what follows, we argue the importance of collecting better data for better outcomes. By better data, we mean a greater emphasis on inclusive research design, implementation, and analysis practices that enable the disaggregated examination of distributional effects as well as the recentering of psychological, in addition to behavioral, outcomes in our research. By better outcomes, we emphasize the central lens of equity. We intentionally propose practices that are applicable to the broader field of psychological science, given its foundational role in the design of behavioral science interventions, as well as applied behavioral insights, where these interventions are scaled to diverse and large populations. These guidelines will enable social psychology to more meaningfully and responsibly engage with applied domains, particularly public policy, with the aim of promoting equitable, in addition to efficient and cost-effective, insights.

5.1 Need for Disaggregated Data

Social psychology as a field is largely motivated by the desire to draw generalizable conclusions about human psychology and behavior in an aim to document universalist truths. However, our current research practices and norms are not well-tailored to reliably draw such conclusions. Scholars have argued that this reality reveals the biases of our field. First, this bias manifests in the way that our data are designed and collected – a prevalence of WEIRD qualities across participants, procedures, context, and scholars (Henrich et al., 2010; Nzinga et al., 2018) as well as a prioritization for internal over external validity (Sue, 2000). Second, research that examines disaggregated effects or prioritizes non-default populations is often considered less rigorous, less objective, or less scientific relative to research on default (primarily WEIRD) populations (Nzinga et al., 2018; S. O. Roberts et al., 2020). Nzinga and colleagues further highlight that the lack of emphasis on disaggregated data is not present in all fields. Indeed, sociological work examining the distributional and intersectional effects of organizational efforts to promote diversity documents how different social identity groups are supported or further harmed depending on the intervention selected (Dobbin & Kalev, 2016; Kalev et al., 2006). Findings suggest that some efforts, such as grievance systems, may be particularly harmful or detrimental to Asian men and less so to White women, while other efforts, such as diversity task forces, may be more supportive of Black women but less so for Black men (Dobbin & Kalev, 2016). Thus, understanding the distributional effects enables a better examination of the underlying factors that may be driving divergent outcomes across different identities.

Moreover, when a disease or treatment outcome is not examined in particular communities, there is often societal pressure placed on institutions, such as the National Institutes of Health in the United States, or similar public entities, to increase the representativeness of the science (for a more detailed argument, see Nzinga et al., 2018). These pressures have been noted in the current efforts to understand the disaggregated and distributional effects of COVID-19, across health consequences, treatment, and prevention. These same social and scientific pressures have not been present in social psychological research. As noted in Section 4, much of the science published in US-based journals does not, as common practice, include basic demographic information about the participants in that research. As such, universalist claims absent the supporting data are problematic for social psychology as a discipline and precarious when social psychological insights are applied to other domains and contexts. Furthermore, as "Big Data" analytic practices become more commonplace throughout the social sciences, it will be increasingly important to consider the design and implementation of these techniques, as acknowledged and discussed in a recent review of so-called hypernudging practices (Yeung, 2016). Around the world, the extent to which individuals engage in digital environments continues to increase, inviting new opportunities to design specialized behavioral interventions. This must be done with strict attention to both ethics and privacy.

In addition to ethical implications, these realities matter for our science. Research across several varying contexts highlights the heterogeneity of psychological and behavioral outcomes that can be elicited by similar contexts. In the context of cognition, social considerations are key. Individuals' perceptions of perceived fundamental cognitions have been shown to vary as a function of social category membership. Henrich and colleagues (2010) provide an overview of the numerous contexts in which social categories and context predict variation in psychology and behavior, including but not limited to visual perception, distribution of resources in economic decision-making, and social cognition and cooperation (see also Henrich, 2015). From a cultural perspective, examining distinction across cultural contexts has been significant for the field. Critical work in social psychology documenting distinctions in decision-making across East Asian and US contexts pushed the field and its understanding (Markus & Kitayama, 1991; Nisbett & Masuda, 2003). Though the impact of interdependent and independent cultural and societal contexts on decision-making, social perception, and behavior appears fundamental to the field today, this was not initially the case and provided an important step toward building cultural context.

This cultural variation is present within WEIRD contexts as well, underscoring the ability and need to further examine the role and intersection of social and demographic constructs. For example, while Western contexts are perceived to prioritize independence and agency, such preferences vary across subgroup categories. One set of studies demonstrated that the act of making a choice and the meaning ascribed to it has differential significance to individuals as a function of their social class membership. In particular, individuals from working-class backgrounds were more likely to express a normative preference for similarity to others in their choices and experience positive affect when others made the same choice they had made, while individuals from middle-class backgrounds were more likely to prefer appearing different from others and experience negative or ambivalent emotions when others made the same choice as they had (Stephens et al., 2007). We acknowledge that social class, as with many social categories, is a continuum and context-dependent. Individuals who are objectively well-off can still feel disadvantaged (Chou et al., 2016; Mani et al., 2013). While taking this into account, we still contend there is value in social psychology building nuance in our understanding. Studies such as those discussed here are a critical positive step in that direction. The implications of these findings for nudging and behavioral science applications are significant, particularly when considering paradigms that aim to elicit active choice and utilize social norms to shift behavior.

In addition to basic research in social cognition and cultural variation, reactions to applications of social psychology to the public policy domain also vary by context and individual factors. For example, perceived political framing of nudges shifts their perceived ethicality, with nudges that align with participants' political orientation being viewed more favorably than those that do not (Tannenbaum et al., 2017). Jung and Mellers (2016) examined attitudes toward nudges that targeted either System 1 (automatic, unconscious processes) or System 2 (conscious, deliberative) decision-making and identified distributional effects on support for such efforts along demographic and individual difference measures. In particular, US attitudes were overall favorable toward the application of behavioral science interventions when these applications emphasized education interventions and reminders (System 2) compared to defaults (System 1). However, these preferences varied as a function of participants' personality traits (desire for control, empathy, reactant), sociocultural orientation (individualistic; see also Hagman et al., 2015), and political orientation.

Consistent with this finding, public attitudes toward nudging, while overall positive, were rated more favorably in a sample of Swedish participants relative to US participants and garnered greater support from people with more analytical, compared to intuitive, mindsets (Hagman et al., 2015). These examinations of broader public support for the utilization of social psychological findings to applied contexts exemplify the complexity of applying social psychological phenomena and theory to applied domains.

Separately, given that race, gender, and other sociodemographic categories are social constructs, such considerations should play a key role in social psychological research and application. More often, however, race (Nzinga et al., 2018; Rad et al., 2018; S. O. Roberts et al., 2020), other sociodemographic factors, individual differences (DeJesus et al., 2019; Nzinga et al., 2018; Rad et al., 2018; Rozin, 2001), and culture more broadly (Brady et al., 2018) are rarely mentioned in our journals. For example, between 1970 and 2018, approximately 5 percent of empirical (with human subjects) articles published in six prominent social and cognitive psychology journals highlighted race, via an examination of the title, abstract, and participant information (S. O. Roberts et al., 2020). While this number has increased over the five-decade span, the overall proportion remains low despite the significant variation in lived experiences as a function of race, for example. The above-cited scholars argue that researchers should begin to provide more detail on the racial demographics of their samples, justify the demographics of the samples that they choose to use, provide information on constraints regarding the generalizability of findings, and include positionality statements – making clear how the identity of authors relates to the topic being studied. We provide our own set of recommendations regarding data disaggregation and believe that they are compatible and complementary with these suggestions.

5.1.1 Recommendations for Disaggregating Data

To understand the psychological and behavioral outcomes of applied social psychology we make the following recommendations:

Disaggregate Participant Data

A first step to understanding the distributional effects of social psychological phenomena is to examine the distribution and variability of participants and participant characteristics in our research. Social psychology reliably documents and considers gender differences in research (Rad et al., 2018), and these same practices should be expanded to additional sociodemographic and cultural factors.

Do So Intentionally

To date, much of the data examining behavioral outcomes fails to disaggregate and intentionally examine the impacts of behavioral outcomes. This is, in part, due to a lack of prioritization of such effects and greater prioritization of norms of universality and generalizability. As a result, experiments are often under-powered to statistically examine subsample effects and processes. Indeed, the framing of research itself must shift – from a perception that an effect is universal unless proven otherwise to the perspective that researchers have the onus of demonstrating universality – and that phenomena are context-dependent until compelling and rigorously collected data suggest otherwise (Simons et al., 2017). We echo the call of numerous scholars to make our science less WEIRD (DeJesus et al., 2019; Henrich, 2015; Nzinga et al., 2018; Rad et al., 2018) by justifying and accounting for the samples selected in social psychological research (S. O. Roberts et al., 2020). Social psychology has a practical and ethical responsibility to theorize about, design, and collect data with intentionality that allows researchers to draw conclusions and develop systematic research projects. Disaggregating data should not simply be a post hoc practice conducted with underpowered datasets where nondominant groups are minimally represented. Just as we justify our sample sizes and preregister our analysis plans, so too must disaggregating our data become a central lens through which social psychological research is conducted – across the spectrum, from scholars examining individual differences to those aiming to establish universality.

5.2 Collect Data in Enriched Contexts

The cross-domain impact of social psychology has increased markedly in recent decades. This includes clear applications to business and management disciplines, private sector application, as well as public administration and policy domains. These include local, state, provincial, and national government agencies (e.g., the Lab@DC, OES, LabGob, etc.), public sector consultants, think tanks, and nonprofits across social and environmental domains. Social psychologists are called upon to engage these considerations directly when developing their lines of research and seeking out grant support for that research. For example, the National Science Foundation in the United States requires researchers to explicitly identify and articulate the broader impacts of their work, including clearly communicating the value of the research for promoting social good and the increased representation of research participants and scholars. Social psychologists are well positioned to answer this call. Much of our work directly emphasizes examining social living and promoting social welfare and this work has clear translations to applied domains. To do this work more equitably, and examine the lived social experiences of individuals and groups across contexts, we need to enrich the contexts we examine.

Prominent scholars in social psychology have noted the field's relative emphasis on internal validity over external validity. This emphasis results in a significant limitation of the science – making it less applicable and inclusive as a consequence. In his breakup letter with the field, Robert Cialdini noted that the field has de-emphasized the role and significance of field work – research conducted in applied contexts and environments on naturally occurring behavior (Cialdini, 2009). Such shifts in emphasis and revolutions within the field make it more challenging to publish research that steps outside of normative and default practices – particularly for research on underrepresented or marginalized identities (Sue, 2000) and among junior scholars pursuing tenure and promotion (Cialdini, 2009). Moreover, our practices of preferring multiple, highly controlled experiments with large sample sizes have the impact of limiting the participation of less well-resourced scholarship.

While in the broader sense large sample sizes will be necessary to conduct cross-sectional and subgroup analyses that enable disaggregation of data, we do introduce a consequence of this, and thus, a caveat. In particular, the overrepresentation of dominant groups in convenience samples (i.e., the large representation of White students at most universities and in online participant pools) means that it is easier (less effortful, less costly, and more efficient) to recruit the required number of participants to meet a priori power analysis recommendations in a manner that biases the inclusion of dominant groups. As such, the demands of recruiting enough participants to complete experiments that will meet the publication standards of our field favors recruiting from dominant samples. However, the underrepresentation of marginalized groups in convenience samples means that there is a tension in place – a need to better understand these historically underrepresented experiences is coupled with a reality in which the lower representation means the data will be seen as less valuable. Indeed, other scholars have noted the relative devaluation of scholarship that examines marginalized group members' experiences – only serving to further marginalize these identities (Hartmann et al., 2013; Nagayama Hall & Maramba, 2001). To the extent that our public spaces and spaces of higher learning remain inequitable and are plagued by systemic inequities, these tensions persist. This, in conjunction with the limited inclusion of field work and naturally occurring behavior, has limited the ability for non-elite institutions to substantively engage and make contributions to the research field. And there are direct consequences for the application of social psychology to other domains. In particular, if policymakers have the potential to favor nudges over more substantive policy initiatives (Hagmann et al., 2019) and yet most individuals are not represented in those behavioral insights data and are likely (presently and historically) the communities most negatively affected by policies, this can build cycles of inequity.

Expanding the contexts in which we examine social psychological phenomena beyond the laboratory or computer has both intellectual and equity benefits. Geographical variation, cultural variation, and within-culture distinctions provide important context and caveats to generalized findings about human behavior. Including culture and data collected outside of the lab significantly increases the interpretive power of the field. Brady and colleagues (2018) note the importance of incorporating culture into our theory and research practices, as doing so enables the field to more accurately understand people's psychological experiences and behavioral outcomes). One avenue to increase such interpretive power is through conducting environmentally and contextually rich experiments in the field, where behavior naturally occurs or where there is the opportunity to test such science in the wild.

5.2.1 Recommendations for Examining Enriched Contexts

We do not anticipate or recommend that social psychology abandon the benefits of internal validity. Indeed, these controlled-environment studies have proved meaningful and monumentally contributed to our understanding of human psychology, social cognition, and behavior. We do, however, recommend that basic and applied social psychologists incorporate research practices that promote external validity – that the field acknowledge the inherent value of triangulating around phenomena using multiple and mixed methodologies.

Enrich the Lab Environment

As a field, we seek to understand how the real, imagined, or anticipated presence of others interacts with our physical and social environments. Where possible, we recommend social psychology incorporate more realistic and psychologically immersive environments for research participants. This can be achieved in laboratory and online settings using available technologies and tools, including more realistically mimicking the participation of real others, development and integration of study confederates, and developing protocols and practices where decisions carry consequences and outcomes that can be applied to the external environment. To address some research questions, it is essential to recruit diverse, community participants to lab settings to participate in research studies (as opposed to solely relying on traditional college student populations). For example, research on financial decision-making would be best served by the recruitment of participants who make these choices on a daily basis – which is not the case for many, if not most, students in traditional college settings.

Step Outside the Lab

To do justice to the endeavor of incorporating enriched environments, we must also examine social phenomena in the contexts in which they occur. Given research practices that promote multiple experiments or studies to support claims and hypothesis testing, we recommend researchers pursue one study or experiment outside of the lab or virtual environment. This entails thoughtfully identifying environments that present opportunities to examine the phenomenon in context and adapting study materials to be relevant to the context. Indeed, researchers do this in the lab – examining research questions and hypotheses across varied lab-based scenarios. An extension of this effort enables meaningful testing of generalizability and boundary conditions in our research and provides important caveats and contingencies for applied behavioral insights.

Do So Ethically

Of critical import are the practices implemented to sustain these recommended efforts. Indeed, stepping outside the lab to collect data in context and from traditionally underrepresented samples has the unfortunate, though realistic, potential for exploitation of these populations. Psychology, along with other social and behavioral sciences, has a documented history of examining diverse samples as part of conscious and intentional efforts to solidify racial hierarchies and white supremacy (see Guthrie, 1976; Winston, 2011). The potential for scholars from Western and dominant cultures to recruit participants and conduct scholarship in relatively underrepresented spaces introduces concern of power differentials and dynamics, the potential for exploitation, a failure to adequately account for the lived experiences and psychologies of the population and context, and thus the ability to reify biases and systemic inequities in our science. Indeed, many communities are weary of academic interventions that fail to engage local cultures, ways of knowing, values, and perspectives. Diversifying our field is not, on its own, a sufficient pathway to a more equitable science and application of research. In efforts to stymie these detrimental effects, the APA, as one governing body of social psychology, has offered guidelines that underscore the key considerations of race, ethnicity, and multicultural responsiveness, as well as socioeconomic status, as broad but fundamental lenses and further offers research-specific frames to consider. From a fundamental perspective, psychologists are called on to establish baseline and continuing education on racial, ethnic, and global perspectives in their own perspectives and their work. Moreover, there is normative pressure to examine personal positionality in the professional, racial, and sociocultural hierarchy and the values and biases that stem from that positionality (APA, 2017, 2019a, 2019b).

6 Conclusion

6.1 Additional Considerations from Behavioral Insights Interventions

When considering behavioral science applications to applied domains, it is worth noting some important realities of behavioral science interventions that can help us understand when and where they work best. First, it has been demonstrated that these interventions often have quite small effect sizes, requiring large samples to demonstrate their effectiveness. In many cases, however, this tradeoff is perfectly acceptable – especially when considering interventions at a very large scale that are truly small in cost. For example, a simple implementation intentions prompt was successful at increasing influenza vaccination rates by about 4 percent. This finding was statistically significant, of course, but also consequential from a practical perspective (Milkman et al., 2011).

In addition, much of the basic and applied research generated by social psychologists and other researchers relies on self-report data or observed behavior and behavioral intentions. In contrast, much of the work in public policy application of behavioral insights relies on administrative data to measure the impact of interventions, which is often difficult to access and exceptionally difficult to alter data collection for. In the United States, this is in part due to the Paperwork Reduction Act (PRA),[7] which requires that government agencies must obtain approval from the Office of Management and Budget (OMB) before engaging with most forms of information from the public. The PRA protects members of the public from being overwhelmed by requests for information from the government (which is certainly a net benefit to the public). But the OMB approval process can be quite cumbersome, creating challenges to conducting social science research in the context of the actions of the government. As such, the applied domain's large reliance on administrative data to implement and measure the impact of these effects means that it is often near impossible to integrate features such as personalization in their design. More importantly, the challenges of administrative data also mean that a deep examination of impacts on subgroups is difficult. Often, governments (at both the local and the federal level) do not have access to the data that will easily allow for disaggregation of the effects of an intervention.

There is also evidence that general support for these practices is sensitive to political affiliation. Across different policy contexts, people find nudges to be acceptable when they are illustrated by examples that align with their political

---

[7] Paperwork Reduction Act (44 U.S.C. 3501 et seq.), https://digital.gov/resources/paperwork-reduction-act-44-u-s-c-3501-et-seq/.

preferences – but view them as unethical when the examples go against their politics. The effect goes away when that context is removed (Tannenbaum et al., 2017). However, other scholars examining nudges in the context of several European nations do not find a significant relationship between party affiliation and support for nudges or other psychological outcomes, though they note nation-level differences in support (Hornsey et al., 2018; Reisch & Sunstein, 2016; Sunstein et al., 2018), and others have argued that, in the context of the United States, nudges are supported across political parties because they align with the progressive, social welfare values of liberals and the fiscal responsibility values of conservatives (Cialdini, 2018). This suggests that practitioners should take a nuanced look when trying to understand support for (or opposition to) behavioral interventions.

Another area of opportunity is a deeper understanding of the persistence of behavioral interventions. Some interventions seem to produce longer-term changes, while others disappear as soon as the treatment ceases. Some researchers have provided an excellent framework for understanding the distinction and describe four pathways hypothesized to impact treatment persistence: building psychological habits, changing what (and how) people think, adjusting future costs, and harnessing external reinforcement (Frey & Rogers, 2014). Their approach to understanding intervention persistence is particularly useful from a policy perspective, where the potential societal benefits (and costs) of these approaches are often quite significant. Overall, we know that these approaches do have the potential to change behavior in the service of overall well-being, but there seems to be variation across contexts.

6.2 Concluding Thoughts

As noted in Sections 2.2 and 2.3, the first significant wave of applied social psychology to public policy began more than a decade ago and with it came the growth and incorporation of behavioral insights to significant social problems. There has been a great deal of policies and applied practices generated from these initial efforts to apply social psychological science to other domains and disciplines. The domain of applied behavioral insights is now at an inflection point. At a recent conference discussion that both authors attended, we engaged in conversation with scholars, researchers, and practitioners using behavioral insights to examine critical public policy dilemmas. The theme of the discussion was clear: there is a need to move beyond documenting the presence of decision-making challenges to identifying strategies to mitigate these boundaries in the public domain. This theme was consistent with the call put out by Milkman and colleagues (2009) more than a decade ago for behavioral insights scholars to move beyond identifying decision-making errors or biases to providing tools and practices that improved people's decision-making.

Moreover, government employees, public sector consultants, and academics all agreed – to do so we need to move the field of applied behavioral insights in the direction of deliberately and extensively considering social identities, contexts, and cultural variation in order to address social problems. Beyond understanding people's biases, we need to be able to help address them with ethical, culturally informed, representative, and equitable processes and practices. This is a call that social psychology is uniquely well-suited to answer. Distinct from behavioral economics or other related domains, social psychology integrates and sits at the intersection of sociodemographic factors, environment, and cultural nuance and we care deeply about attitudes, behaviors, and cognitions that shape our daily lives with a scope far beyond economic decisions. These conversations have largely happened in parallel. However, decades of theory have been developed in social psychology, and from this foundation, researchers are well positioned to build and test boundaries and universals, with intentional increases in participant, context, and cultural representation.

Indeed, moving beyond the relatively low-hanging fruit of documenting biases to understanding the complexity of individual difference and social-cultural factors in predicting psychological and behavioral outcomes around such decision-making and behavioral biases is crucial. Doing so asserts basic and applied social psychology's relevance to cross-disciplinary and cross-sector efforts aimed at understanding and promoting the social good. The preceding sections document the consequences and potential costs of failing to do so. These include developing behavioral interventions at scale that overlook the crucial consideration of psycho-emotional outcomes, in addition to behavior change. Applied behavioral insights has emphasized behavior change efforts, while not recognizing that pairing psychological outcomes enables a more complete understanding of the potential costs of nudging, as well as tools for more sustainable and effective interventions. Indeed, some scholars and academics have begun to recognize the importance of such considerations given recent work examining personalized nudges (Mills, 2022; Ruggeri et al., 2020) that target behavior change by emphasizing individual preferences. In addition, we emphasized the importance of examining distributional effects of applied behavioral insights.

The one-size-benefits-all approach that has been largely utilized in the field is no longer applicable as we look to the next phase of behavioral insights. If our science continues to favor and prioritize dominant groups, there will be broad and significant implications for applied domains integrating our findings into their work. The inequities that this has the potential to perpetuate should give the field pause. Understanding the distributional effects is central to developing a field that promotes equitable treatment of and benefits to individuals. This is all the more crucial a consideration given that existing examinations of distributional effects highlight a significant concern: that individuals who are relatively disadvantaged in the given domain or context are those that bear the cost (Auferoth, 2020; Ghesla et al., 2020; Thunström, 2019; Thunström et al., 2018). Thus, there is the possibility that many applications of behavioral insights benefit those already better off (Thunström 2019; Thunström et al., 2018) and harm those who would benefit most from the nudge, or that the effects of such interventions swing wider for underserved populations (e.g. Mrkva et al., 2021). For social psychology to authentically engage as an equitable science, one that identifies universal principles and context-dependent behavioral and psychological outcomes that aim to understand the human condition, we need to bring an increased awareness and intentionality to our efforts. Indeed, "a willful neglect of study sample variability represents an abdication of a fundamental moral and scientific principle" (Nzinga et al., 2018, p. 11440). We offer that, if nudges are to be costless, the next wave of applied behavioral insights must consider the psychological and distributional costs in addition to existing considerations of economic costs.

We began this Element with an excerpt from President Obama's Executive Order on using insights from behavioral science. One section of that order reads as follows:

> To more fully realize the benefits of behavioral insights and deliver better results at a lower cost for the American people, the Federal Government should design its policies and programs *to reflect our best understanding of how people engage with, participate in, use, and respond to those policies and programs.* (emphasis added)

Without deep consideration of these psychological, behavioral, and economic costs, we will never fully realize the "best understanding" referenced here. It is in the interest of the public good for us to do better.

References

Abrahamse, W., & Steg, L. (2013). Social influence approaches to encourage resource conservation: A meta-analysis. *Global Environmental Change, 23*(6), 1773–1785. https://doi.org/10.1016/j.gloenvcha.2013.07.029

Allcott, H. (2011). Social norms and energy conservation. *Journal of Public Economics, 95*(9), 1082–1095. https://doi.org/10.1016/j.jpubeco.2011.03.003

Allcott, H. (2016). Paternalism and energy efficiency: An overview. *Annual Review of Economics, 8*(1),145–176. https://doi.org/10.1146/annurev-economics-080315-015255

Allcott, H., & Kessler, J. B. (2019). The welfare effects of nudges: A case study of energy use social comparisons. *American Economic Journal: Applied Economics, 11*(1), 236–276. https://doi.org/10.1257/app.20170328

Allcott, H., & Mullainathan, S. (2010). Behavior and energy policy. *Science, 327*(5970), 1204–1205. https://doi.org/10.1126/science.1180775

Allcott, H., & Rogers, T. (2014). The short-run and long-run effects of behavioral interventions: Experimental evidence from energy conservation. *American Economic Review, 104*(10), 3003–3037. https://doi.org/10.1257/aer.104.10.3003

Angawi, A. F., & Hasanain, W. A. (2018). The nuts and bolts of behavioral insights units. In A. Samson, ed., *The Behavioral Economics Guide 2018* (pp. 24–35). Behavioral Science Solutions. www.behavioraleconomics.com/be-guide/the-behavioral-economics-guide-2018/

APA (American Psychological Association). (2017). *Multicultural Guidelines: An Ecological Approach to Context, Identity, and Intersectionality, 2017.* www.apa.org/about/policy/multicultural-guidelines

APA (American Psychological Association). (2019a). *APA Guidelines on Race and Ethnicity in Psychology.* www.apa.org/about/policy/guidelines-race-ethnicity.pdf

APA (American Psychological Association). (2019b). *APA Guidelines for Psychological Practice for People with Low-Income and Economic Marginalization.* www.apa.org/about/policy/guidelines-low-income.pdf

Arnett, J. J. (2008). The neglected 95%: Why American psychology needs to become less American. *American Psychologist, 63*(7), 602–614. https://doi.org/10.1037/0003-066X.63.7.602

Arno, A., & Thomas, S. (2016). The efficacy of nudge theory strategies in influencing adult dietary behaviour: A systematic review and meta-analysis. *BMC Public Health, 16*(676). https://doi.org/10.1186/s12889-016-3272-x

Auferoth, F. (2020). Who benefits from nudges for exam preparation? An experiment. SSRN Scholarly Paper ID 3424583. Social Science Research Network. https://doi.org/10.2139/ssrn.3424583

Axt, J. R. (2018). The best way to measure explicit racial attitudes is to ask about them. *Social Psychological and Personality Science*, 9(8), 896–906. https://doi.org/10.1177/1948550617728995

Benartzi, S., Beshears, J., Milkman, K. L. et al. (2017). *Should governments invest more in nudging? Psychological Science*, 28(8), 1041–1055. https://doi.org/10.1177/0956797617702501

Beshears, J., Choi, J., Laibson, D., Madrian, B., & Weller, B. (2010). Public policy and saving for retirement: The "autosave" features of the Pension Protection Act of 2006. In J. J. Siegfried, ed., *Better Living through Economics* (pp. 274–290). Cambridge, MA: Harvard University Press.

Bos, A. E. R., Pryor, J. B., Reeder, G. D., & Stutterheim, S. E. (2013). Stigma: Advances in theory and research. *Basic and Applied Social Psychology*, 35(1), 1–9. https://doi.org/10.1080/01973533.2012.746147

Brady, L. M., Fryberg, S. A., & Shoda, Y. (2018). Expanding the interpretive power of psychological science by attending to culture. *Proceedings of the National Academy of Sciences*, 115(45), 11406–11413. https://doi.org/10.1073/pnas.1803526115

Broers, V. J. V., De Breucker, C., Van den Broucke, S., & Luminet, O. (2017). A systematic review and meta-analysis of the effectiveness of nudging to increase fruit and vegetable choice. *European Journal of Public Health*, 27(5), 912–920. https://doi.org/10.1093/eurpub/ckx085

Byerly, H., Balmford, A., Ferraro, P. J. et al. (2018). Nudging pro-environmental behavior: Evidence and opportunities. *Frontiers in Ecology and the Environment*, 16(3), 159–168. https://doi.org/10.1002/fee.1777

Cadario, R., & Chandon, P. (2019). Which healthy eating nudges work best? A meta-analysis of field experiments. *Marketing Science*, 39(3), 465–486. https://doi.org/10.1287/mksc.2018.1128

Camerer, C. F. (1998). *Prospect Theory in the Wild: Evidence from the Field*. Report No. 1037. California Institute of Technology. https://resolver.caltech.edu/CaltechAUTHORS:20170811-150835361

Ceci, S. J., Kahan, D. M., & Braman, D. (2010). The WEIRD are even weirder than you think: Diversifying contexts is as important as diversifying samples. *Behavioral and Brain Sciences*, 33(2–3), 87–88. https://doi.org/10.1017/S0140525X10000063

Chou, E. Y., Parmar, B. L., & Galinsky, A. D. (2016). Economic insecurity increases physical pain. *Psychological Science*, 27(4), 443–454. https://doi.org/10.1177/0956797615625640

Cialdini, R. B. (2009). We have to break up. *Perspectives on Psychological Science, 4*(1), 5–6. https://doi.org/10.1111/j.1745-6924.2009.01091.x

Cialdini, R. B. (2018). Why the world is turning to behavioral science. In A. Samson, ed., *The Behavioral Economics Guide 2018* (pp. 77–14). Behavioral Science Solutions. www.behavioraleconomics.com/be-guide/the-behavioral-economics-guide-2018/

Clark, W. A. V., & Lisowski, W. (2017). Prospect theory and the decision to move or stay. *Proceedings of the National Academy of Sciences, 114*(36), E7432–E7440. https://doi.org/10.1073/pnas.1708505114

Cohen, J. (1988). *Statistical Power Analysis for the Behavioral Sciences*, 2nd ed. Hillsdale, NJ: Lawrence Erlbaum Associates.

Congdon, W. J., & Shankar, M. (2015). The White House Social & Behavioral Sciences Team: Lessons learned from year one. *Behavioral Science & Policy, 1*(2), 77–86. https://doi.org/10.1353/bsp.2015.0010

Corrigan, P. W., & Lam, C. (2007). Challenging the structural discrimination of psychiatric disabilities: Lessons learned from the American disability community. *Rehabilitation Education, 21*(1), 53–58. https://doi.org/10.1891/088970107805059869

Cortland, C. I., Shapiro, J. R., Guzman, I. Y., & Ray, L. A. (2019). The ironic effects of stigmatizing smoking: Combining stereotype threat theory with behavioral pharmacology. *Addiction, 114*(10), 1842–1848. https://doi.org/10.1111/add.14696

Dede, O. Ç. (2019). Behavioral policies and inequities: The case of incentivized smoking cessation policies. *Journal of Economic Methodology, 26*(3), 272–289. https://doi.org/10.1080/1350178X.2019.1625223

DeJesus, J. M., Callanan, M. A., Solis, G., & Gelman, S. A. (2019). Generic language in scientific communication. *Proceedings of the National Academy of Sciences, 116*(37), 18370–18377. https://doi.org/10.1073/pnas.1817706116

DellaVigna S., & Linos E. (2022). RCTs to scale: Comprehensive evidence from two nudge units. *Econometrica, 90*(1), 81–116.

Dobbin, F., & Kalev, A. (2016). Why diversity programs fail. *Harvard Business Review*, July 1. https://hbr.org/2016/07/why-diversity-programs-fail

Dupree, C. H., & Kraus, M. W. (2022). Psychological science is not race neutral. *Perspectives on Psychological Science, 17*(1), 270–275. https://doi.org/10.1177/1745691620979820

Emmons, D. L., Mazzuchi, T. A., Sarkani, S., & Larsen, C. E. (2018). Mitigating cognitive biases in risk identification: Practitioner checklist for the aerospace sector. *Defense Acquisition Research Journal, 25*(1), 52–93. https://doi.org/10.22594/dau.16-770.25.01

Esmark, A. (2019). Communicative governance at work: How choice architects nudge citizens towards health, wealth and happiness in the information age. *Public Management Review, 21*(1), 138–158. https://doi.org/10.1080/14719037.2018.1473476

Ewert, B. (2020). Moving beyond the obsession with nudging individual behaviour: Towards a broader understanding of Behavioural Public Policy. *Public Policy and Administration, 35*(3), 337–360. https://doi.org/10.1177/0952076719889090

Eyal, N. (2014). Nudge, embarrassment, and restriction: Replies to Voigt, Tieffenbach, and Saghai. *International Journal of Health Policy and Management, 4*(1), 53–54. https://doi.org/10.15171/ijhpm.2015.01

Fine, B., Johnston, D., Santos, A. C., & Waeyenberge, E. V. (2016). Nudging or fudging: The World Development Report 2015. *Development and Change, 47*(4), 640–663. https://doi.org/10.1111/dech.12240

Fong, G. T., Hammond, D., & Hitchman, S. C. (2009). The impact of pictures on the effectiveness of tobacco warnings. *Bulletin of the World Health Organization, 87*, 640–643. www.who.int/bulletin/volumes/87/8/09-069575/en/

Frey, E., & Rogers, T. (2014). Persistence: How treatment effects persist after interventions stop. *Policy Insights from the Behavioral and Brain Sciences, 1*(1), 172–179. https://doi.org/10.1177/2372732214550405

Ghesla, C., Grieder, M., & Schubert, R. (2020). Nudging the poor and the rich: A field study on the distributional effects of green electricity defaults. *Energy Economics, 86*(C). https://ideas.repec.org/a/eee/eneeco/v86y2020ics014098831930413x.html

Gigerenzer, G. (2015). On the supposed evidence for libertarian paternalism. *Review of Philosophy and Psychology, 6*(3), 361–383. https://doi.org/10.1007/s13164-015-0248-1

Glaeser, E. L. (2005). Paternalism and psychology. Working Paper No. w11789. National Bureau of Economic Research. https://doi.org/10.3386/w11789

Guthrie, R. V. (1976). *Even the Rat Was White: A Historical View of Psychology.* New York: Harper & Row.

Haeffel, G. J., & Howard, G. S. (2010). Self-report: Psychology's four-letter word. *The American Journal of Psychology, 123*(2), 181–188. https://doi.org/10.5406/amerjpsyc.123.2.0181

Hagman, W., Andersson, D., Västfjäll, D., & Tinghög, G. (2015). Public views on policies involving nudges. *Review of Philosophy and Psychology, 6*(3), 439–453. https://doi.org/10.1007/s13164-015-0263-2

Hagmann, D., Ho, E. H., & Loewenstein, G. (2019). Nudging out support for a carbon tax. *Nature Climate Change, 9*(6), 484–489. https://doi.org/10.1038/s41558-019-0474-0

Hall, C. C., Zhao, J., & Shafir, E. (2014). Self-affirmation among the poor: Cognitive and behavioral implications. *Psychological Science*, *25*(2), 619–625. https://doi.org/10.1177/0956797613510949

Hansen, P. G. (2016). The definition of nudge and libertarian paternalism: Does the hand fit the glove? *European Journal of Risk Regulation*, *7*(1), 155–174. https://doi.org/10.1017/S1867299X00005468

Harmeling, C. M., Mende, M., Scott, M. L., & Palmatier, R. W. (2021). Marketing, through the eyes of the stigmatized. *Journal of Marketing Research*, 58(2), 223–245. https://doi.org/10.1177/0022243720975400

Hartmann, W. E., Kim, E. S., Kim, J. H. J. et al. (2013). In search of cultural diversity, revisited: Recent publication trends in cross-cultural and ethnic minority psychology. *Review of General Psychology*, *17*(3), 243–254. https://doi.org/10.1037/a0032260

Hatzenbuehler, M. L., & Link, B. G. (2014). Introduction to the special issue on structural stigma and health. *Social Science & Medicine*, *103*, 1–6. https://doi.org/10.1016/j.socscimed.2013.12.017

Hauser, O. P., Gino, F., & Norton, M. I. (2018). Budging beliefs, nudging behaviour. *Mind & Society*, *17*(1), 15–26. https://doi.org/10.1007/s11299-019-00200-9

Hausman, D., & Welch, B. (2010). Debate: To nudge or not to nudge. *Journal of Political Philosophy*, *18*(1), 123–136. https://doi.org/10.1111/j.1467-9760.2009.00351.x

Hebda, C., & Wagner, J. (2016). Nudging healthy food consumption and sustainability in food deserts. *Letters in Spatial and Resource Sciences*, *9*(1), 57–71. https://doi.org/10.1007/s12076-015-0138-2

Helweg-Larsen, M., Sorgen, L. J., & Pisinger, C. (2019). Does it help smokers if we stigmatize them? A test of the stigma-induced identity threat model among U.S. and Danish smokers. *Social Cognition*, *37*(3), 294–313. https://doi.org/10.1521/soco.2019.37.3.294

Hemphill, J. F. (2003). Interpreting the magnitude of correlation coefficients. *American Psychologist*, *58*(1), 78–79.

Henrich, J. (2015). Culture and social behavior. *Current Opinion in Behavioral Sciences*, *3*, 84–89. https://doi.org/10.1016/j.cobeha.2015.02.001

Henrich, J., Heine, S. J., & Norenzayan, A. (2010). The weirdest people in the world? *The Behavioral and Brain Sciences*, *33*(2–3), 61–83; discussion 83–135. https://doi.org/10.1017/S0140525X0999152X

Hornsey, M. J., Harris, E. A., & Fielding, K. S. (2018). Relationships among conspiratorial beliefs, conservatism and climate scepticism across nations. *Nature Climate Change*, *8*(7), 614–620. https://doi.org/10.1038/s41558-018-0157-2

Hummel, D., & Maedche, A. (2019). How effective is nudging? A quantitative review on the effect sizes and limits of empirical nudging studies. *Journal of Behavioral and Experimental Economics*, *80*, 47–58. https://doi.org/10.1016/j.socec.2019.03.005

John, P. (2014). Policy entrepreneurship in UK central government: The behavioural insights team and the use of randomized controlled trials. *Public Policy and Administration*, *29*(3), 257–267. https://doi.org/10.1177/09520767135 09297

John, P., Smith, G., & Stoker, G. (2009). Nudge nudge, think think: Two strategies for changing civic behaviour. *The Political Quarterly*, *80*(3), 361–370. https://doi.org/10.1111/j.1467-923X.2009.02001.x

Johnson, E. J., & Goldstein, D. (2003). Do defaults save lives? *Science*, *302*(5649), 1338–1340.

Jung, J. Y., & Mellers, B. A. (2016). American attitudes toward nudges. *Judgment and Decision Making*, *11*(1), 13.

Kahneman, D. (2011). *Thinking, Fast and Slow*. New York: Macmillan.

Kahneman, D., & Tversky, A. (1979). Prospect theory: An analysis of decision under risk. *Econometrica*, *47*(2), 263–291. https://doi.org/10.2307/1914185

Kalev, A., Dobbin, F., & Kelly, E. (2006). Best practices or best guesses? Assessing the efficacy of corporate affirmative action and diversity policies. *American Sociological Review*, *71*(4), 589–617. https://doi.org/10.1177/000312240607100404

Keating, S. (2018). The nation that thrived by "nudging" its population. *BBC*, February 20. www.bbc.com/future/article/20180220-the-nation-that-thrived-by-nudging-its-population

Kirakozian, A. (2016). One without the other? Behavioural and incentive policies for household waste management. *Journal of Economic Surveys*, *30*(3), 526–551. https://doi.org/10.1111/joes.12159

Krendl, A. C., & Pescosolido, B. A. (2020). Countries and cultural differences in the stigma of mental illness: The East–West divide. *Journal of Cross-Cultural Psychology*, *51*(2), 149–167. https://doi.org/10.1177/0022022119901297

Levy, D. E., Riis, J., Sonnenberg, L. M., Barraclough, S. J., & Thorndike, A. N. (2012). Food choices of minority and low-income employees: A cafeteria intervention. *American Journal of Preventive Medicine*, *43*(3), 240–248. https://doi.org/10.1016/j.amepre.2012.05.004

Lewis, M. (2016). *The Undoing Project: A Friendship That Changed Our Minds* (illustrated ed.). New York: W. W. Norton & Company.

Loewenstein, G., & O'Donoghue, T. (2006). "We can do this the easy way or the hard way": Negative emotions, self-regulation, and the law. *The University of Chicago Law Review*, *73*(1), 183–206.

Madrian, B. C., & Shea, D. F. (2001). The power of suggestion: Inertia in 401(k) participation and savings behavior. *The Quarterly Journal of Economics*, *116*(4), 1149–1187. https://doi.org/10.1162/003355301753265543

Major, B., Hunger, J. M., Bunyan, D. P., & Miller, C. T. (2014). The ironic effects of weight stigma. *Journal of Experimental Social Psychology, 51*, 74–80. https://doi.org/10.1016/j.jesp.2013.11.009

Mani, A., Mullainathan, S., Shafir, E., & Zhao, J. (2013). Poverty impedes cognitive function. *Science, 341*(6149), 976–980. https://doi.org/10.1126/science.1238041

Marchiori, D. R., Adriaanse, M. A., & De Ridder, D. T. D. (2017). Unresolved questions in nudging research: Putting the psychology back in nudging. *Social and Personality Psychology Compass, 11*(1), e12297. https://doi.org/10.1111/spc3.12297

Markus, H. R., & Kitayama, S. (1991). Culture and the self: Implications for cognition, emotion, and motivation. *Psychological Review, 98*(2), 224–253. https://doi.org/10.1037/0033-295X.98.2.224

McKenzie, C. R. M., Liersch, M. J., & Finkelstein, S. R. (2006). Recommendations implicit in policy defaults. *Psychological Science, 17*(5), 414–420. https://doi.org/10.1111/j.1467-9280.2006.01721.x

Milfont, T. L., & Markowitz, E. (2016). Sustainable consumer behavior: A multilevel perspective. *Current Opinion in Psychology, 10*, 112–117. https://doi.org/10.1016/j.copsyc.2015.12.016

Milkman, K. L., Beshears, J., Choi, J. J., Laibson, D., & Madrian, B. C. (2011). Using implementation intentions prompts to enhance influenza vaccination rates. *Proceedings of the National Academy of Sciences, 108*(26), 10415–10420. https://doi.org/10.1073/pnas.1103170108

Milkman, K. L., Chugh, D., & Bazerman, M. H. (2009). How can decision making be improved? *Perspectives on Psychological Science, 4*(4), 379–383. https://doi.org/10.1111/j.1745-6924.2009.01142.x

Mills, S. (2020). Nudge/sludge symmetry: On the relationship between nudge and sludge and the resulting ontological, normative and transparency implications. *Behavioural Public Policy*, 1–24. https://doi.org/10.1017/bpp.2020.61

Mills, S. (2022). Personalized nudging. *Behavioural Public Policy, 6*(1), 150–159.

Mols, F., Haslam, S. A., Jetten, J., & Steffens, N. K. (2015). Why a nudge is not enough: A social identity critique of governance by stealth. *European Journal of Political Research, 54*(1), 81–98. https://doi.org/10.1111/1475-6765.12073

Mrkva, K., Posner, N. A., Reeck, C., & Johnson, E. J. (2021). Do nudges reduce disparities? Choice architecture compensates for low consumer knowledge.

Journal of Marketing, 0022242921993186. https://doi.org/10.1177/0022242
921993186

Muthukrishna, M., Bell, A. V., Henrich, J. et al. (2020). Beyond Western, educated, industrial, rich, and democratic (WEIRD) psychology: Measuring and mapping scales of cultural and psychological distance. *Psychological Science, 31*(6), 678–701. https://doi.org/10.1177/0956797620
916782

Muthukrishna, M., & Henrich, J. (2019). A problem in theory. *Nature Human Behaviour, 3*(3), 221–229. https://doi.org/10.1038/s41562-018-0522-1

Nagayama Hall, G. C., & Maramba, G. G. (2001). In search of cultural diversity: Recent literature in cross-cultural and ethnic minority psychology. *Cultural Diversity and Ethnic Minority Psychology, 7*(1),12–26. https://doi
.org/10.1037/1099-9809.7.1.12

Nisbett, R. E., & Masuda, T. (2003). Culture and point of view. *Proceedings of the National Academy of Sciences, 100*(19), 11163–11170. https://doi.org/
10.1073/pnas.1934527100

Nisbett, R. E., & Wilson, T. D. (1977). Telling more than we can know: Verbal reports on mental processes. *Psychological Review, 84*(3), 231–259. https://
doi.org/10.1037/0033-295X.84.3.231

Nzinga, K., Rapp, D. N., Leatherwood, C. et al. (2018). Should social scientists be distanced from or engaged with the people they study? *Proceedings of the National Academy of Sciences, 115*(45), 11435–11441. https://doi.org/
10.1073/pnas.1721167115

OECD (Organisation for Economic Co-operation and Development). (2017). *Behavioural Insights and Public Policy: Lessons from around the World.* Paris: OECD Publishing. https://doi.org/10.1787/9789264270480-en

OECD (Organisation for Economic Co-operation and Development). (2019). *Tools and Ethics for Applied Behavioural Insights: The Basic Toolkit.* Paris: OECD Publishing. https://doi.org/10.1787/9ea76a8f-en

OES (Office of Evaluation Sciences). (2019). Using social norms to decrease energy use in public housing. OES abstract. https://oes.gsa.gov/assets/
abstracts/1808%20-%20Project%20Abstract%20HUD%20Energy.pdf

Osbaldiston, R., & Schott, J. P. (2012). Environmental sustainability and behavioral science: Meta-analysis of proenvironmental behavior experiments. *Environment and Behavior, 44*(2), 257–299. https://doi.org/10.1177/00139
16511402673

Petticrew, M., Maani, N., Pettigrew, L., Rutter, H., & Schalkwyk, M. C. V. (2020). Dark nudges and sludge in big alcohol: Behavioral economics, cognitive biases, and alcohol industry corporate social responsibility. *The Milbank Quarterly, 98*(4), 1290–1328. https://doi.org/10.1111/1468-0009.12475

Rad, M. S., Martingano, A. J., & Ginges, J. (2018). Toward a psychology of Homo sapiens: Making psychological science more representative of the human population. *Proceedings of the National Academy of Sciences*, *115* (45), 11401–11405. https://doi.org/10.1073/pnas.1721165115

Reisch, L. A., & Sunstein, C. R. (2016). Do Europeans like nudges? SSRN Scholarly Paper ID 2739118. Social Science Research Network. https://doi .org/10.2139/ssrn.2739118

Richard, F. D., Bond, C. F., & Stokes-Zoota, J. J. (2003). One hundred years of social psychology quantitatively described. *Review of General Psychology*, *7*(4), 331–363. https://doi.org/10.1037/1089-2680.7.4.331

Richburg-Hayes, L., Anzelone, C., & Dechausay, N. (2017). Nudging change in human services: Final report of the Behavioral Interventions to Advance Self-Sufficiency (BIAS) Project. SSRN Scholarly Paper ID 3007745. Social Science Research Network. https://papers.ssrn.com/abstract=3007745

Roberts, J. L. (2018). Nudge-proof: Distributive justice and the ethics of nudging. *Michigan Law Review*, *116*(6), 1045.

Roberts, S. O., Bareket-Shavit, C., Dollins, F. A., Goldie, P. D., & Mortenson, E. (2020). Racial inequality in psychological research: Trends of the past and recommendations for the future. *Perspectives on Psychological Science*, *15*(6), 1295–1309. https://doi.org/10.1177/1745691620927709

Rozin, P. (2001). Social psychology and science: Some lessons from Solomon Asch. *Personality and Social Psychology Review*, *5*(1), 2–14. https://doi.org/ 10.1207/S15327957PSPR0501_1

Ruggeri, K., Benzerga, A., Verra, S., & Folke, T. (2020). A behavioral approach to personalizing public health. *Behavioural Public Policy*, 1–13. https://doi .org/10.1017/bpp.2020.31

Schmidt, A. T., & Engelen, B. (2020). The ethics of nudging: An overview. *Philosophy Compass*, *15*(4), e12658. https://doi.org/10.1111/phc3.12658

Schultz, P. W., Nolan, J. M., Cialdini, R. B., Goldstein, N. J., & Griskevicius, V. (2007). The constructive, destructive, and reconstructive power of social norms. *Psychological Science*, *18*(5), 429–434. https://doi.org/10.1111/ j.1467-9280.2007.01917.x

Sheeran, P., Maki, A., Montanaro, E. et al. (2016). The impact of changing attitudes, norms, and self-efficacy on health-related intentions and behavior: A meta-analysis. *Health Psychology*, *35*(11), 1178–1188. https://doi.org/ 10.1037/hea0000387

Shephard, D. D., Hall, C. C., & Lamberton, C. (2020). Increasing identification of homeless students: An experimental evaluation of increased communication incorporating behavioral insights. *Educational Researcher*, 0013189X209 81067. https://doi.org/10.3102/0013189X20981067

Shih, M., & Sanchez, D. T. (2009). When race becomes even more complex: Toward understanding the landscape of multiracial identity and experiences. *Journal of Social Issues, 65*(1), 1–11. https://doi.org/10.1111/j.1540-4560.2008.01584.x

Simmons, J. P., Nelson, L. D., & Simonsohn, U. (2011). False-positive psychology: Undisclosed flexibility in data collection and analysis allows presenting anything as significant. *Psychological Science, 22*(11), 1359–1366. https://doi.org/10.1177/0956797611417632

Simon, H. A. (1957). *Models of Man; Social and Rational*. New York: Wiley.

Simons, D. J., Shoda, Y., & Lindsay, D. S. (2017). Constraints on generality (COG): A proposed addition to all empirical papers. *Perspectives on Psychological Science, 12*(6), 1123–1128. https://doi.org/10.1177/1745691617708630

Stephens, N. M., Fryberg, S. A., Markus, H. R., Johnson, C. S., & Covarrubias, R. (2012). Unseen disadvantage: How American universities' focus on independence undermines the academic performance of first-generation college students. *Journal of Personality and Social Psychology, 102*(6), 1178–1197. https://doi.org/10.1037/a0027143

Stephens, N. M., Markus, H. R., & Townsend, S. S. M. (2007). Choice as an act of meaning: The case of social class. *Journal of Personality and Social Psychology, 93*(5), 814–830.

Sue, S. (2000). Science, ethnicity, and bias: Where have we gone wrong? *The American Psychologist, 54*(12), 1070–1077. https://doi.org/10.1037/0003-066X.54.12.1070

Sunstein, C. R. (2014). *Simpler: The Future of Government* (reprint ed.). Simon & Schuster.

Sunstein, C. R. (2020). Sludge audits. *Behavioural Public Policy*, 1–20. https://doi.org/10.1017/bpp.2019.32

Sunstein, C. R. (2021). *Sludge: What Stops Us from Getting Things Done and What to Do about It*. Cambridge, MA:MIT Press.

Sunstein, C. R., Reisch, L. A., & Rauber, J. (2018). A worldwide consensus on nudging? Not quite, but almost. *Regulation & Governance, 12*(1), 3–22. https://doi.org/10.1111/rego.12161

Syed, M., Santos, C., Yoo, H. C., & Juang, L. P. (2018). Invisibility of racial/ethnic minorities in developmental science: Implications for research and institutional practices. *American Psychologist, 73*(6), 812–826. https://doi.org/10.1037/amp0000294

Tannenbaum, D., Fox, C. R., & Rogers, T. (2017). On the misplaced politics of behavioural policy interventions. *Nature Human Behaviour, 1*(7), 1–7. https://doi.org/10.1038/s41562-017-0130

Thaler, R. H. (2016). *Misbehaving: The Making of Behavioral Economics* (reprint ed.). New York: W. W. Norton & Company.

Thaler, R. H. (2018). Nudge, not sludge. *Science, 361*(6401), 431. https://doi .org/10.1126/science.aau9241

Thaler, R. H., & Sunstein, C. R. (2003). Libertarian paternalism. *Behavioral Economics, 93*(2), 5.

Thaler, R. H., & Sunstein, C. R. (2009). *Nudge: Improving Decisions about Health, Wealth, and Happiness* (rev. and extended ed.). London: Penguin Books.

Thunström, L. (2019). Welfare effects of nudges: The emotional tax of calorie menu labeling. *Judgment and Decision Making, 14*(1), 11–25.

Thunström, L., Gilbert, B., & Ritten, C. J. (2018). Nudges that hurt those already hurting: Distributional and unintended effects of salience nudges. *Journal of Economic Behavior & Organization, 153*, 267–282. https://doi .org/10.1016/j.jebo.2018.07.005

Tieffenbach, E. (2014). On the cost of shame comment on "nudging by shaming, shaming by nudging." *International Journal of Health Policy and Management, 3*(7), 409–411. https://doi.org/10.15171/ijhpm.2014.125

Vlaev, I., King, D., Dolan, P., & Darzi, A. (2016). The theory and practice of "nudging": Changing health behaviors. *Public Administration Review, 76*(4), 550–561. https://doi.org/10.1111/puar.12564

Wakefield, M. A., Hayes, L., Durkin, S., & Borland, R. (2013). Introduction effects of the Australian plain packaging policy on adult smokers: A cross-sectional study. *BMJ Open, 3*(7). https://doi.org/10.1136/bmjopen-2013-003175

Winston, A. S. (2011). Value neutrality and SPSSI: The quest for policy, purity, and legitimacy. *Journal of Social Issues, 67*(1), 59–72. https://doi.org/ 10.1111/j.1540-4560.2010.01683.x

World Bank. (2014). *World Development Report 2015: Mind, Society, and Behavior.* The World Bank. https://doi.org/10.1596/978-1-4648-0342-0

Wright, M. C., Borbolla, D., Waller, R. G. et al. (2019). Critical care information display approaches and design frameworks: A systematic review and meta-analysis. *Journal of Biomedical Informatics, 100*(3), 100041. https:// doi.org/10.1016/j.yjbinx.2019.100041

Yeung, K. (2017). "Hypernudge": Big Data as a mode of regulation by design. *Information, Communication & Society, 20*(1), 118–136. https://doi.org/ 10.1080/1369118X.2016.1186713

Acknowledgments

The authors would like to thank the Behavioral insights Applied to public Policy (BAP) reading group and Social Policy and Identity Research (SPIR) research assistants at the University of Washington, Evans School of Public Policy and Governance for their research support, feedback, and encouragement of this Element. We also thank Heather Kappes for reviewing earlier drafts.

Cambridge Elements $^{\equiv}$

Applied Social Psychology

Susan Clayton
College of Wooster, Ohio

Susan Clayton is a social psychologist at the College of Wooster in Wooster, Ohio. Her research focuses on the human relationship with nature, how it is socially constructed, and how it can be utilized to promote environmental concern.

About the Series
Many social psychologists have used their research to understand and address pressing social issues, from poverty and prejudice to work and health. Each Element in this series reviews a particular area of applied social psychology. Elements will also discuss applications of the research findings and describe directions for future study.

Cambridge Elements ≡

Applied Social Psychology

Elements in the Series

Printed in the United States
by Baker & Taylor Publisher Services

Printed in the United States
by Baker & Taylor Publisher Services